From Tide To Table

Everything You Ever Wanted To Know About Buying, Preparing and Cooking Seafood

Georgina Campbell

First Published 2008 by

EPICURE PRESS

P.O. Box 6173, Dublin 13.

Text: joint copyright Georgina Campbell & Bord Iascaigh Mhara (BIM)

Photographs: copyright Bord Iascaigh Mhara (BIM)

Drawings: copyright Scandinavian Fishing Year Book (www.scandfish.com)

ISBN 978-1-903164-27-3

A.O
641.692

Editor: Georgina Campbell

Recipe Editor: Orla Broderick

Producer Profiles: Biddy White Lennon

Home Economist: Sharon Hearne-Smith

Food Assistant: Karen Convery

Design: Brian Darling, The Design Station, Dublin

Food Photography: Paul Sherwood (plus images on pages 168/169 and 172 which are courtesy of BIM);

Images on pages 9, 11 and 14 by Terry McDonagh; Back cover by WM Nixon; All other photographs courtesy of BIM

Photographic props kindly supplied by: Avoca, Brown Thomas and Murphy Sheehy Fabrics

AUTHOR ACKNOWLEDGMENTS

Many thanks to all at Bord Iascaigh Mhara (BIM), the Irish Sea Fisheries Board, for their generous support of this book, for sharing recipes and information, and for their keen interest and assistance throughout the project. And thanks also, of course, to all who have worked on it with such enthusiasm - especially Orla Broderick for making the recipes so user-friendly, Sharon Hearne-Smith and Karen Convery for cooking and presenting them beautifully for photography, Paul Sherwood for capturing them on film in natural light and Brian Darling for his design work. And special thanks to Paul's family for putting up with the disruption during the shoot.

Georgina Campbell

October, 2008.

Printed and bound in Spain

Contents

Foreword

As a small island nation on Europe's western seaboard, Ireland's beautifully varied coastline and bountiful seas are – whether we are aware of it on a day to day basis or not – crucial to our very essence. Visitors to this country certainly recognise this and, as well as enjoying the scenery to the full – notably the rugged western seaboard, where the pure Atlantic waters are responsible for some of our finest catches – they value very highly the fresh fish and seafood on offer in our restaurants, hotels and pubs.

Irish people also appreciate seafood when dining out, yet we tend to be reluctant to cook fish at home. I think this is mainly because the very attributes that make fish so well suited to restaurant kitchens – notably the quick last minute cooking, which is ideal for cooking fresh ingredients to order when all the sauces and accompaniments are ready to go - can sometimes make it seem daunting at home, where we are not always so well organised. I think that this book will help to make home cooks feel a lot more confident about cooking fish because the recipes are wide ranging, and offer something for every occasion from everyday family meals to special occasions, yet they are very clear and

straightforward. Also - and very importantly, I feel — we have included an extensive choice of side dishes and accompaniments, including the many sauces and extras that make all the difference to seafood. The dishes have been prepared for photography with their suggested accompaniments, and there are variations and alternative combinations suggested with many of the recipes too, making meal planning very easy.

Seafood is one of the healthiest and most versatile foods available and I hope that, by giving you the knowhow and confidence to cook fish at home, 'From Tide to Table' will make it a favourite in your kitchen.

Georgina Campbell

Georgina Campbell

Introduction

Welcome to Ireland's first ever 'seafood bible', *From Tide to Table*, which is supported by Bord Iascaigh Mhara (BIM), the Irish Sea Fisheries Board. This essential guide tells you everything you've always wanted to know about choosing, preparing and cooking Irish seafood at home.

Luscious Dublin Bay prawns, succulent smoked salmon, mussels and oysters that taste of the sea, chunky monkfish, tasty mackerel, and gorgeous lobster and crab... just a few examples of the delicious seafood you'll find on fish counters and menus all around Ireland. Irish people love to eat seafood when dining out; in fact, unlike our European neighbours, we eat more seafood outside the home than at our own tables. Perhaps this is a testament to the quality of our restaurants – fast-cooked ultra-fresh seafood is certainly the ideal restaurant food, as it can be prepared to order so quickly and simply, and then served up in minutes, in perfect condition. Yet, whilst the number of Irish people consuming fish has increased in recent years, many of us do not include enough fish in our diet, mainly due to the fact that we find the thought of preparing and cooking fish at home daunting – fish is perceived as difficult to cook when in fact it is easy, quick and very versatile.

But don't worry – help is at hand. This book is designed to provide you with all the information you need to know about fish and seafood, including the many health benefits of fish, species identification, buying and storing, the simple facts on responsible fishing and farmed seafood – and a great range of easy-to-follow recipes, including some from leading Irish restaurants and members of the BIM Seafood Circle. In addition to delicious recipes and top tips, this 'seafood bible' also includes features on different types of fishing, and stories of local businesses and the innovative people who have made them successful. From mussel farming in Clew Bay to the history of the Dublin Bay Prawn, from Clare Island Organic Salmon farming to crabbing off Hook Head, there won't be much that you don't know about fish and fishing by the time you have finished this book.

Heritage

Ireland is a small island on the western seaboard of Europe with a long, indented coastline – and nowhere in Ireland are you more than 100km from the sea. The sea, and access to its resources, has always been of prime importance to the population and middens containing heaps of discarded sea shells mark many sites of early occupation.

The ways in which we have utilised our precious fish and shellfish resources down through the ages have changed dramatically, the emphasis has now firmly shifted to ways of management and cultivation. Many people in coastal communities will remember a very different life, in the days of local harvesting – often working by hand to harvest shellfish, or using small rowing boats for inshore fishing – and have seen the changeover to developed

aquaculture, the mechanical harvesting of shellfish and the use of large trawlers that stay at sea for many days. It's a far cry from Molly Malone – who, if she existed at all, was probably just a typical Dublin fisher girl of her time and immortalised in song around 1880.

Fish, the Superfood

Apart from its great taste and versatility in cooking, fish is a real superfood: it is the ultimate fast food, and one of the healthiest too. For example, we have known for decades that people who eat fish have a lower risk of heart disease – but did you know that eating fish at least once a week can cut your chances of a fatal heart attack by more than 50%? Regular consumption of fish is also linked to the prevention of medical conditions as varied as Alzheimer's disease and stroke – claims which are backed by international research.

But fish has a lot more going for it than protection against disease – it's a powerhouse of good nutrition, helping the body to get many of the nutrients it can easily miss out on. Fish is low in fat and rich in protein, which is needed for strong muscles and a healthy immune system, skin and hair. Fish is also rich in iodine, zinc and selenium – essential nutrients that are not found in many other foods: iodine is needed for a healthy metabolism; zinc is necessary for healthy skin and the immune system; and selenium is one of nature's most powerful antioxidants. Fish is also a rich source of several essential vitamins, notably B vitamins which are found in almost all fish – one portion of fish will provide your full day's requirement for vitamin B12. Oil-rich fish are also excellent sources of vitamins A and D: vitamin A promotes healthy skin and good eyesight and vitamin D helps the body to absorb calcium from food. We normally get vitamin D from sunshine, but if the skies are grey you may be running low; eating oil-rich fish is an excellent way to build up your reserves.

And, as if all that is not enough, oil-rich fish are among the best sources of Omega-3 fats. These essential fats are needed for healthy brain development during pregnancy and childhood, and they also help to protect the brain from decline in old age. Omega-3 fats also help to keep skin healthy and may play a role in helping to prevent a wide range of conditions, from dyslexia and ADHD to Type 1 diabetes and asthma.

So it is with good reason that nutritionists recommend that we eat fish at least twice a week – and include oil-rich fish at least once a week. At last: a food we love that's also good for us!

Fish for Growing Children

Easy to digest and a rich source of the protein which is essential for growing bones and muscles, fish has many special benefits to offer children. As well as providing minerals like zinc, selenium and iodine that healthy bones, muscles and immune systems need, the Omega-3 fats found in oil-rich fish such as trout, salmon and mackerel are essential for brain development. Over 60% of the brain is made up of fat, and Omega-3 fats make up about half of this. It is important for young children to eat plenty of Omega-3 fats as our bodies cannot make them and they are only found in a few foods.

It can take time for children (and adults) to get used to the new taste and texture of fish, so do offer it at least once a week. As they get more familiar with the feeling of fish in their mouths, children will start to be more comfortable eating it. It pays to be patient. Start with very small amounts of fish, even a mouthful with a meal, and gradually work up. It generally takes about 6 weeks of trying a new food to become comfortable with it, so take your time.

Getting Kids to Eat Fish – Top Tips

▷ Do start with white fish like whiting and haddock which have a milder flavour. As your child gets used to the fish you can add in new varieties and start introducing the stronger tasting oil-rich fish

▷ Do eat fish yourself. Most children will copy what they see their parents doing – if they see you eating and enjoying fish, they are more likely to try it themselves

▷ Do offer fish to children as early as possible. But take care to remove all the bones, especially the small, fine bones

▷ Do get older children involved in cooking and preparing meals with fish – many children are willing to eat anything they have cooked themselves

▷ Do try lots of different kinds of fish and different ways of cooking them.

▷ Don't force children to eat fish – this usually puts them off. Do encourage them to try even one small taste each time you serve fish and let them eat more if they want it

Ireland's Fisheries – a Precious Resource

Ireland's marine resources are precious and, in an era when the global marine environment is under pressure, we can no longer take the bountiful harvest of the sea for granted. In recent years, there has been an emphasis on developing an environmentally responsible approach to fishing and the conservation of our valuable marine resources.

Good management of wild fisheries is the key to sustainability. The systems that are now in place, including EU rules on quotas for the landing of certain varieties of fish, have assisted in the protection of dwindling fish stocks. Innovative fishing methods reduce the number of unwanted bycatch (other fish caught in nets whilst fishing for a particular species) and of undersized fish, and prevent over-fishing to ensure that the fish population in the waters remains at sustainable levels.

Bord Iascaigh Mhara (BIM), the Irish Sea Fisheries Board is currently working with the Irish seafood sector to help promote and develop a more responsible and sustainable industry. This includes encouraging and promoting best practice, developing new methods to reduce bycatch, promoting continuous improvement in technology used in fishing, aquaculture and processing to minimise the environmental impact and encouraging retailers and restaurants to buy responsibly sourced seafood through the Seafood Circle initiative. BIM has already worked with the industry on a number of successful initiatives aimed at improving sustainability including the Lobster V-notching programme that consists of fishermen marking immature lobsters with a small v-notch in the tail and returning them alive to the sea so other fishermen can see at a glance that the lobster is immature and must be returned. There has been progress made on inshore management, and waste management, which requires fishermen to comply with a system for the collection and recycling of old netting. There is also an initiative called 'Deepclean' which aims to recover lost nets at sea that continue to catch fish or 'ghost-fish' as they drift along the bottom of the sea. There are also a number of initiatives to improve Ireland's fishing fleets from an environmental management perspective, including technical conservation measures and improved fuel efficiency.

For further information on the above initiatives and to learn more about responsible fishing visit **www.bim.ie**

Farmed Seafood – a Healthy Alternative

Not all fish come from wild fisheries. There has been a growth in the number of cultivated oysters, mussels and clams, and in the farming of trout, Arctic charr and salmon. Stocks of traditional wild species have dwindled, but farmed seafood now offers a sustainable and healthy alternative.

Currently there are BIM Irish Quality Seafood schemes for salmon, organic salmon, mussels, trout and oysters, and a specific Eco-certification for mussels and salmon. Each Quality Scheme ensures that the product adheres to the highest standards from the hatchery to packing and that the fish or shellfish has been hatched, reared, harvested and packed under strict rules relating to food hygiene. For example, a certified mussel has stringent product specification on meat content, shell appearance, taste and texture, and has been produced and processed by companies that operate best practice in food safety, employee and environmental welfare. The entire supply chain is covered.

The BIM Irish Quality Eco-Standard is awarded to farmers and processors who meet strict environmental criteria and guarantees that the product has been produced with due care for the environment above and beyond existing legal requirements. The Eco-Standard, which currently applies to mussels and salmon, is independently accredited.

Irish Farmed Salmon – A Quality Product

Irish farmed salmon has an excellent reputation worldwide for its high quality, and there are a number of reasons for this. Irish conditions are unique: grown in huge sea pens, the fish density is low with 98% of the volume in the pens being fast-moving seawater in exposed coastal sites where the fish swim the equivalent of 23,000km in the eighteen months they spend growing to market size. Their primary diet is fishmeal produced from fresh, wholefish trimmings, and the pigments used to allow salmon to develop pink flesh are naturally occurring pigments called carotenoids (which also give carrots their colour); they are essential nutrients for salmon and identical to those that make wild salmon pink. All regulations relating to salmon farming are stringent, emphasising sustainability and independent accreditation, thus ensuring that the standards needed to grow superior quality salmon are maintained.

BIM Seafood Circle
Irish Seafood… Something Special

Seafood is incredibly versatile, allowing chefs and home cooks alike to create innovative dishes suitable for all occasions whether it's breakfast, light lunch, a quick snack or a special dinner. BIM has developed the Seafood Circle initiative to support and reward restaurateurs and retailers offering top quality seafood and service to their customers. There are three strands to the programme — Hospitality, Supermarket Seafood Counters and Seafood Specialist — and a growing number of members in each category.

Visitors to Ireland place a high value on the range and quality of Irish seafood — for many, a trip to Ireland wouldn't be complete without sampling a few oysters and sinking a pint of the black stuff. Locally caught seafood is especially good and is often flagged on the menu — and, of course, it is widely available to home cooks, who can also benefit from the range of seafood and expertise offered by Seafood Circle retail members. So look out for Seafood Specialists and Supermarket Seafood Counter members, who offer a wide selection of top quality fresh seafood, invitingly displayed — and served by pleasant, courteous staff with good knowledge of how to prepare and cook seafood.

Check out the listings on **www.seafoodcircle.ie** and you'll find the establishments currently carrying the distinctive Seafood Circle logo. Seafood Circle membership is awarded on an annual basis and may be withdrawn at any stage if an establishment fails to continue to meet the criteria necessary

Buying and Storing Seafood
Recommendations for Buying Irish Seafood

For the benefit of the consumer, it is a legal requirement for all fresh and frozen fish to be labelled with the catch area and production method (i.e. wild or farmed), so don't forget to ask your fishmonger where the product you are buying was farmed, or the region from which it was caught.

Buying locally caught or farmed seafood ensures that it reaches you in the freshest condition; that transport, pollution and waste are kept to a minimum; and that local communities are being supported.

Shopping for Seafood Should be an Adventure

▶ Talk to your fishmonger: they are the experts and will be able to advise you what fish is plentiful and offers value for money

▶ Be open to change: if the variety you want isn't available, substitute another. Fish is very versatile and one type can easily be swapped for another in a recipe. Again, your fishmonger will be a mine of valuable information

▶ Freshness is paramount: choose whole fish with bright, prominent shining eyes, bright red or pink gills, distinct skin colour and above all a clean fresh 'sea smell'

▶ Fillets should be translucent with no sign of discolouration

▶ Your fishmonger will be happy to fillet or skin fish if you feel you're not up to the task

▶ Get the fish into the fridge as soon as possible – remember it's highly perishable and must be kept cool Remove any packaging, clean with a damp cloth or kitchen paper and store in a shallow dish at the bottom of the fridge, where it is coldest and there is no danger of dripping onto other foods

▶ Fish is best used on the day of purchase if possible, although it can usually be kept for 24 hours if bought fresh and correctly stored

▶ Mussels and oysters should be stored in a bowl at the bottom of the fridge, covered with a damp cloth or kitchen paper, and cooked within 12 hours

▶ If buying packaged seafood, including smoked and frozen fish, check that the packaging is in good condition, and that it is within the use-by date

Cooking Fish – the Basic Methods

There are various different ways to cook fish, and they are all basically simple; however, as fish cooks quickly and overcooking is the easiest way to spoil it, careful cooking is important.

Restaurants capitalise on the fact that the basic cooking methods are straightforward and quick, with acccurate timing, good sauces and varied accompaniments the secret of their success. Through good planning and advance preparation of accompaniments (see Chapter Eight), home cooks can easily use the same techniques.

The basic cooking methods are all used in recipes in this book; they include grilling/chargrilling, roasting and barbecueing (dry-heat cooking); poaching and steaming (wet-heat cooking) and sautéeing/pan-frying, stir-frying and deep-frying (cooking in oil). Sometimes fish is smoked, 'cooked' without heat by marinating in citrus juice (as in gravadlax), or eaten raw (as in sushi).

Species – *Oil-Rich Fish*

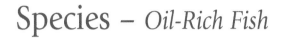

Freshwater Reared Rainbow Trout
Oncorhynchus mykiss • Breac Dea-dhathach Fionnuisce

Arctic Charr
Salvelinus alpinus • Ruabhreac Artach

Mackerel
Scomber scombrus • Ronnach

Salmon
Salmo salar • Bradán

Herring
Clupea harengus • Scadán

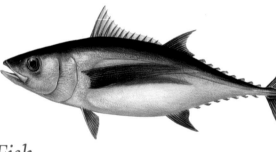

Sea Reared Rainbow Trout
Oncorhynchus mykiss (anadromous)
Breac Dea-dhathach Mara

Albacore Tuna
Thunnus alalunga • Tuinnín Bán

Species – *White Fish*

Hake
Merluccius merluccius • Colmóir

John Dory
Zeus faber • Deoraí

Ling
Molva Molva • Langa

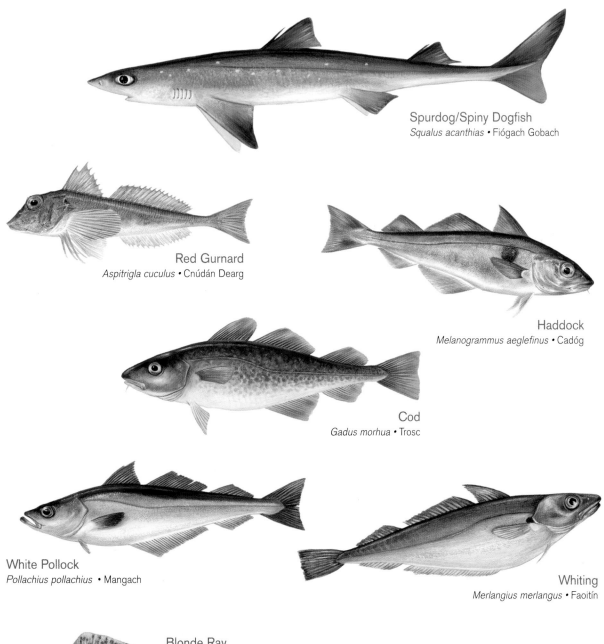

Spurdog/Spiny Dogfish
Squalus acanthias • Fiógach Gobach

Red Gurnard
Aspitrigla cuculus • Cnúdán Dearg

Haddock
Melanogrammus aeglefinus • Cadóg

Cod
Gadus morhua • Trosc

White Pollock
Pollachius pollachius • Mangach

Whiting
Merlangius merlangus • Faoitín

Blonde Ray
Raja brachyura • Roc Fionn

Black Pollock/Coley
Pollachius virens • Glasán

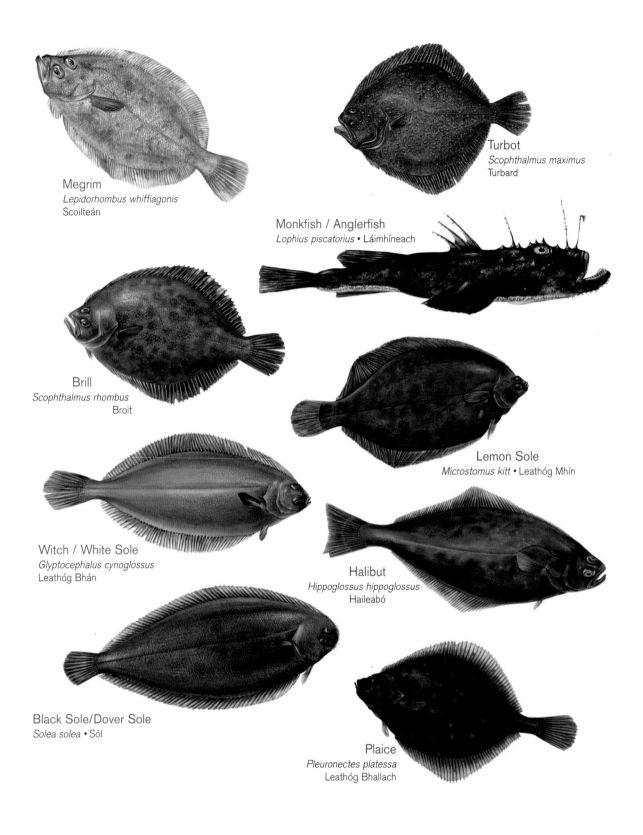

Megrim
Lepidorhombus whiffiagonis
Scoilteán

Turbot
Scophthalmus maximus
Turbard

Monkfish / Anglerfish
Lophius piscatorius • Láimhíneach

Brill
Scophthalmus rhombus
Broit

Lemon Sole
Microstomus kitt • Leathóg Mhín

Witch / White Sole
Glyptocephalus cynoglossus
Leathóg Bhán

Halibut
Hippoglossus hippoglossus
Haileabó

Black Sole/Dover Sole
Solea solea • Sól

Plaice
Pleuronectes platessa
Leathóg Bhallach

Species – *Molluscs & Crustaceans*

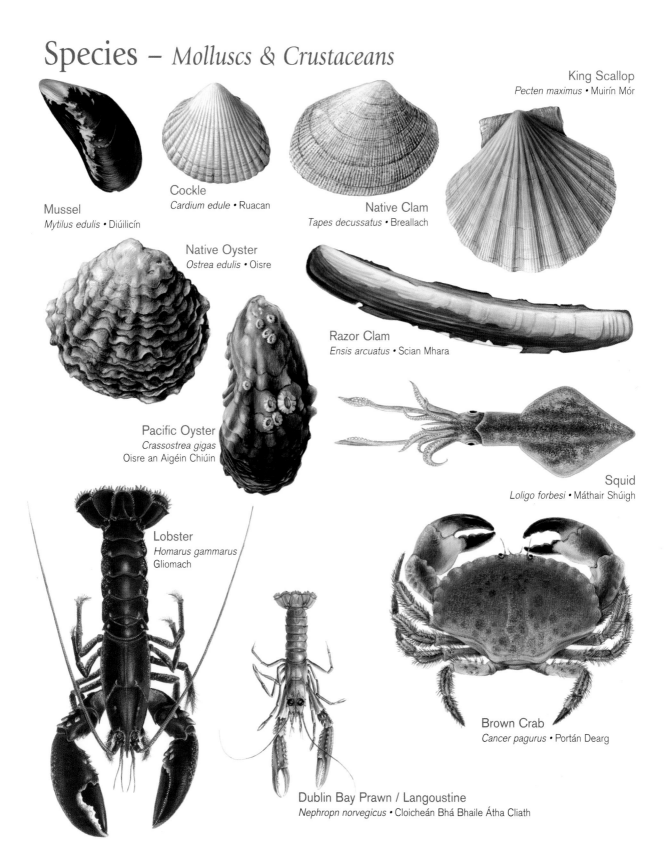

Mussel
Mytilus edulis • Diúilicín

Cockle
Cardium edule • Ruacan

Native Clam
Tapes decussatus • Breallach

King Scallop
Pecten maximus • Muirín Mór

Native Oyster
Ostrea edulis • Oisre

Razor Clam
Ensis arcuatus • Scian Mhara

Pacific Oyster
Crassostrea gigas
Oisre an Aigéin Chiúin

Squid
Loligo forbesi • Máthair Shúigh

Lobster
Homarus gammarus
Gliomach

Brown Crab
Cancer pagurus • Portán Dearg

Dublin Bay Prawn / Langoustine
Nephropn norvegicus • Cloicheán Bhá Bhaile Átha Cliath

Fish & Tips - Know Your Seafood

Fish are broadly classified as FINFISH and SHELLFISH.

FINFISH are divided into white fish and oil-rich fish.

White Fish are sometimes referred to as "lean fish" because all the oils are contained in the liver, which is removed during gutting. White fish are further sub-divided into:
- Round white fish – cod, haddock, hake and pollock
- Flat white fish – plaice, lemon sole, brill, turbot and black sole
- Cartilaginous fish – ray, rock salmon and shark

Oil-Rich Fish get their name from the fact that the oils are distributed throughout the flesh of the fish. Mackerel, herring, salmon and trout are common examples.

Sometimes you will find fish classified in a different way:
- Demersal fish – these fish live on or near the sea bed. Round and flat white fish fall into this category.
- Pelagic fish – swim in mid-waters or near the surface. Oil-rich fish such as mackerel, herring and tuna are examples.

SHELLFISH are broadly divided into two main categories – Molluscs and crustaceans.

Molluscs can be divided into three categories:
- Uni-valve molluscs – those with one shell - periwinkle and whelks.
- Bi-valve molluscs – those with two shells hinged at one end; mussels, oysters and scallops are good examples.
- Cephalopods – this type of shellfish has no outer shell, just a single internal 'pen', squid and cuttlefish.

Crustaceans are more mobile creatures with hard segmented shells and flexible joints. Examples include prawns, shrimp, crab and lobster.

Fish may be offered for sale prepared in various ways.
- Whole ungutted fish should not have burst bellies as this is an indication of spoilage.
- Whole gutted fish should be free of all gut pieces, with clean washed gut cavity. The head may or may not be left on. If the fish is cooked "head-on" the gills should be removed, also every trace of blood along the back bone.
- Steaks and cutlets are made by cutting across the backbone of the fish. Steaks and cutlets should be about 2.5cm/1 inch in thickness and neatly cut. All traces of blood must be removed from steaks/cutlets.
- Butterfly fillet (also known as 'block fillet') is cut from both sides of a fish with the two pieces remaining held together by the skin. Small whiting, herring and mackerel are often filleted in this way.
- Side/single fillet is a slice of flesh removed from one side of a fish by a cut made parallel to the back bone. All fins and bones, with the exception of pin bones, are removed. Cod is usually filleted in this way.
- Darne is a portion of a fillet (e.g. salmon) cut perpendicular to where the backbone used to be.

Certain types of fish are presented for sale as suited to the species:
- Ray is normally sold as wings with the skin removed.
- Monkfish – the head is usually removed and just the tail presented. The skin is normally removed.
- Rock salmon is difficult to fillet and skin. Normally it is presented for sale in lengths (filleted and skinned) with just the central cartilage remaining.
- Squid may be presented with head and tentacles removed and body opened out in a triangular shape.

Preparation – Fish & Seafood

SKINNING & DE-BONING ROUND FISH

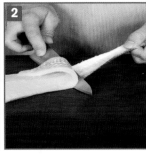

1. Make incision through flesh toward tail

2. Keeping tight grip on skin, work knife in saw-like motion towards top of fillet

3. Remove small 'v' shape of flesh containing bones

TO FILLET FLAT FISH

1. Cut away head in 'v' shape

2. Clean cavity

3. Remove fins

4. Remove first side fillet

5. Turn fish and repeat with second fillet

6. Repeat on underside to remove bottom fillets

SKINNING BLACK SOLE

1. Loosen skin at tail

2. Keeping firm grip, pull skin towards head

3. Repeat on underside

TO SKIN & FILLET MONKTAIL

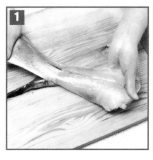

1. Pull skin towards tail
2. Cut fillets from central bone and remove membrane

TO PREPARE WHOLE SALMON

1. Cut out gills
2. Pack washed cavity with crushed foil
3. Place in fish kettle or roasting tin
4. When cooked and cool, peel away skin
5. Remove dark flesh
6. Portion by lifting sections off the bone

TO PREPARE LOBSTER

1. Remove claws
2. Cut away underside shell
3. Remove flesh
4. Remove stomach and discard
5. Crack claws
6. Remove meat from claws

TO OPEN OYSTERS

 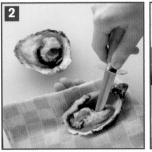

1. Use sturdy flat-bladed knife to separate shells
2. Loosen oyster flesh from shell

TO PREPARE MUSSELS

 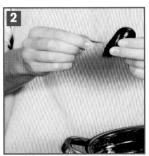

1. Tap mussels to ensure they close. Discard any that remain open
2. Wash well and remove byssus thread by tugging sharply

TO SHELL WHOLE PRAWNS/TAILS

1. Remove head by twisting sharply
2. Break off top section of tail shell
3. Gently pull prawn flesh from remainder of shell

TO PREPARE SQUID

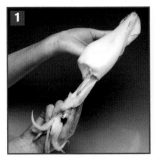 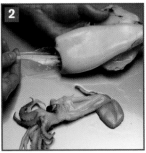 

1. Pull tentacles and head away from body
2. Remove 'pen' and body flaps
3. Cut tentacles from head. Discard remainder

TO OPEN SCALLOPS

1. Separate shells using flat-bladed knife
2. Gently remove contents
3. Separate white meat and coral. Discard all other material

Mussels *no need to seed or feed*

The most abundant, most widespread and most versatile of Irish shellfish, the common or blue mussel (*Mytilus edulis* - or an *diúilicín* in Irish), is to be seen on virtually every rock, pier and rope in the sea around Ireland. A double-shelled mollusc with an inky blue-black curved shell, it is a native shellfish and has been eaten in Ireland since ancient times - and, thanks to Molly Malone, is associated with Ireland throughout the world. Mussels are lazy creatures by nature, attaching themselves in clusters to whatever comes their way with byssus (numerous threads produced by the mussel itself), then they just stay there and filter in the food-rich seawater. Although many methods are used in modern mussel cultivation, the basic principle of growing mussels is simple - give them something to attach themselves to in food-rich water. They grow wild, in or near estuaries and bays, and use a filter system to feed on plankton, taking in up to 45 litres of seawater a day to nourish themselves. Depending on the type of plankton they feed on, their flesh is white or orange in tone.

The oldest method of culturing mussels dates back to the middle ages. It is still used in France today and is said to have been invented by an Irishman called Walton, who was shipwrecked near La Rochelle. Endeavouring to catch wild birds, he attached nets to tall stakes driven into the seabed. When the stakes were examined he found them covered in mussels which were developing remarkably well, and he was clever enough to see he was on to a good thing. The method is still used today in that region of France. Mussels need neither seeding nor feeding. Encourage them to settle in the right place with high quality water rich in nutritious plankton and they will seed naturally and grow, no matter what method you use.

In the 1980's Michael Mulloy began growing mussels in Clew Bay, County Mayo. Although mussels thrive naturally in the sheltered waters of the bay, Michael was a pioneer in this area of aquaculture. Michael explains, "with Class A waters, and in a bay with many islands and shelter, I chose a spot that was convenient and, luckily, it turned out to be a good choice."

Michael Molloy and his business partner John Hensey, drawing ideas from all over the world, have led the way in developing full automation of the husbandry and harvesting of cultured mussels on Blackshell Farm. They are also men with a passion for being kind to the environment. In seawater about 18 metres deep, a natural biodegradable rope up to 5,000 metres in length is laid in repeated U-shaped loops attached at intervals to buoys. Within 2-3 weeks the mussel spawn settles pretty evenly, and within 4 weeks you can see a black column of mussels at a density too high to grow large mussels.

So, the rope is hauled in, the mussels are graded, and then put into a sausage-shaped cotton tube which is replaced in the water, where they naturally reattach themselves with their own threads. This process is repeated about every six months until the mussels are ready for harvesting, in 18-20 months. "We harvest for 10 months of the year and all our mussels are processed nearby. As the water is so good there is no need for purification, it's done naturally."

Almost all of Blackshell Farm's mussels are cooked and frozen, many with sauces, making them into high-value, ready-to-heat-and-eat products. The Irish mussel processing industry is now a world leader in the supply of value-added mussel products that are appreciated by quality-conscious consumers.

It's a long way from Molly Malone wheeling her wheelbarrow crying "cockles and mussels, alive, alive-o".

Soups & Starters

Crab cakes with red pepper & chilli relish

Smokies

Garlic stuffed mussels

Smoked mackerel paté

Smoked salmon on warm potato pancakes with sweet mustard dressing

Galway Bay oysters sashimi-style

Classic prawn cocktail

Greencastle chowder

The Lobster Pot seafood chowder

Razor clams with parsley & garlic

Seared scallops with black pudding, crispy bacon and beurre blanc

Beetroot gravadlax with sweet mustard & dill sauce

Crab Cakes with Coriander and Chilli

These crab cakes are really delicious and very easy to prepare. There really is no alternative to crab meat but do try to use white meat that is in largish chunks rather than lots of little pieces. It is best sourced from a good fishmonger – or, if you have access to fresh crabs, you can of course cook them yourself.

225g/8oz white crab meat,
    thawed if frozen
50g/2oz spring onions, trimmed and
    finely chopped
50g/2oz mayonnaise
75g/3oz fresh white breadcrumbs
1 small egg, lightly beaten
1 tbsp chopped fresh coriander
1 small red chilli, seeded and
    finely chopped
2 tbsp sunflower oil
salt and freshly ground black pepper

To Serve
lightly dressed green salad (page 185)
red pepper and chilli relish (page 198)

SERVES 4

Place the crab meat in a bowl with the spring onions, mayonnaise, breadcrumbs, egg, coriander and chilli. Season to taste and mix gently until well combined. Divide the mixture into eight and then shape into crab cakes.

Heat the oil in a heavy-based frying pan. Add the crab cakes and cook for 3-4 minutes on each side until heated through and golden brown. Arrange the crab cakes on plates with some lightly dressed green salad and a good dollop of the red pepper and chilli relish to serve.

VARIATION
For a more traditional flavour omit the chilli and use parsley instead of coriander.

Smokies

Smoked coley is more easily available than smoked haddock, but haddock is finer in both flavour and texture. It makes a delicious winter soup when the fishing boats can't get out in stormy weather but, for a mouth watering hot starter, you really can't beat this dish.

225g/8oz smoked haddock or cod
        or pollock (undyed if possible)
300ml/½ pint milk
a little finely chopped onion
pinch of freshly ground pepper
2 firm ripe tomatoes
300ml/½ pint cream
50g/2oz red Cheddar cheese, grated
chopped fresh flat-leaf parsley, to garnish

To Serve
freshly baked brown soda bread,
        (page 193)

SERVES 4

Preheat the oven to 190°C/375°F/Gas 5. Put the smoked haddock into a pan with the milk and onion, season with pepper, then bring slowly to the boil. Remove the fish from the milk immediately. Discard the milk; skin the fish, remove any bones and break the flesh up into pieces.

Plunge the tomatoes briefly into boiling water to loosen the skins, then peel, scoop out and discard the seeds and chop the flesh. Divide half of the tomato between four ramekin dishes. Add the smoked haddock, then put the remaining tomato on top. Divide the cream among the dishes, scatter the grated cheese on top and bake for about 20 minutes until golden brown and bubbling. Garnish each dish with a little parsley and serve at once with some brown bread.

Garlic Stuffed Mussels

Mussels are plentiful, good value for money and perfect as a starter, to hand around at parties or just as a snack. Always wash in plenty of cold water and scrub the shells with a stiff brush. Use a knife to scrape off any barnacles. Discard any open mussels that do not close when lightly tapped on the work surface. Pull out the tough, fibrous beards protruding from the tightly closed shells.

1kg/2¼lb fresh mussels
about 50g/2oz coarse rock salt
150g/5oz butter
4 garlic cloves, crushed
1 tbsp chopped fresh flat-leaf parsley
squeeze of fresh lemon juice
25g/1oz fresh white breadcrumbs

To Serve
lemon wedges

SERVES 4

Preheat the grill. Place the mussels in a shallow, heavy-based pan (no liquid is necessary). Cover with a tight fitting lid and cook over a high heat for 3-5 minutes, shaking occasionally until they have opened. (Discard any that do not open.)

Remove the top shell from each mussel and arrange the bottom shell and flesh on a bed of the rock salt in individual ovenproof dishes.

Melt the butter in a small pan; add the garlic, parsley and lemon juice. Add the breadcrumbs and mix well. Place a little of the mixture onto each of the mussels.

Place the garlic stuffed mussels directly under the grill for 3-5 minutes until the breadcrumbs are golden brown. Serve at once with lemon wedges.

VARIATION
You can also make this recipe with clams or cockles.

Smoked Mackerel Paté

This paté is great as a starter, or for serving on canapés when entertaining. It also is a quick and easy snack served on hot toast.

450g/1lb smoked mackerel fillets
75g/3oz cream cheese
75g/3oz crème fraîche
1-2 tbsp creamed horseradish
dash of Tabasco sauce
juice of ½ lemon
salt and freshly ground black pepper

To Serve
selection of crackers and celery sticks

SERVES 4

Remove the skin from the mackerel fillets and discard any bones, then break up the flesh into a bowl. Add the cream cheese, crème fraîche, one tablespoon of the horseradish, the Tabasco and lemon juice. Mix thoroughly until well combined, then taste and add the remaining horseradish, if liked. Season to taste and transfer to a serving bowl.

Set the bowl of smoked mackerel paté on a platter and add a selection of crackers and celery sticks to serve.

VARIATION
Use smoked trout or hot smoked salmon instead of smoked mackerel.

Smoked Salmon on Warm Potato Pancakes with Pickled Red Onion

This tasty combination of smoked salmon and warm potato pancakes has a hint of northern European influence in the pickled red onion accompaniment but, overall, it has a lovely Irish feeling to it - and it has become popular of late, to use as starter or, perhaps, as a light lunch or supper dish.

4 tbsp rice or white wine vinegar
2 tbsp caster sugar
1 small red onion, thinly sliced
250g/9oz floury potatoes, such as
    Rooster
50g/2oz unsalted butter
2 tbsp plain flour
2 eggs, separated
4 tbsp double cream
225g/8oz smoked salmon slices
1 tbsp chopped fresh dill
salt and freshly ground black pepper

To Serve
sweet mustard dressing (page 200)

SERVES 4

To make the pickled red onions: Place the vinegar in a bowl and stir in the sugar and a pinch of salt to dissolve. Add the onion slices and toss to coat. Cover with clingfilm and set aside for at least 10 minutes (or up to 1 hour is fine if time allows), then drain and keep covered with clingfilm in the fridge until ready to use (up to 48 hours is fine).

Place the potatoes in a pan of boiling salted water, cover and simmer for 15-20 minutes until tender. Drain, then return to the pan for a few minutes to dry out. Mash until smooth, using a potato ricer or sieve set over a bowl and pushing the potatoes through with a wooden spoon - this gives a really smooth finish. Beat in 25g/1oz of the butter, then fold in the flour and the egg yolks until just combined. Add the cream, a little at a time until you have achieved a smooth batter. Season to taste.

Heat a flat griddle pan or large frying pan over a gentle heat. Whisk the egg whites in a bowl until soft peaks have formed and then carefully fold into the potato mixture. Add the remaining butter to the pan and, when it has stopped sizzling, spoon on six mounds of the potato mixture. Cook gently for 2-3 minutes on each side, turning once or twice until puffed up and golden brown. Keep warm and repeat with the remaining butter and potato mixture until you have twelve pancakes in total.

Transfer the potato pancakes on to warmed serving plates and arrange the smoked salmon slices on top, then drizzle around the sweet mustard dressing. Stir the dill into the pickled red onion and scatter over each plate to serve.

Galway Bay Oysters Sashimi-Style

This recipe from Kevin Dundon of Dunbrody Country House Hotel and Cookery School, County Wexford, is a great way to introduce oysters to your guests. It is not too difficult to open oysters, they really are quite simple (see below). An oyster knife is a good investment if you are planning to serve oysters regularly.

12 Pacific/Gigas oysters
1 tbsp sesame seeds
about 225g/8oz coarse rock salt
6 tbsp dark soy sauce
finely grated rind and juice of 1 lime
1 tbsp shredded root ginger
1 spring onion, finely shredded
4 tbsp sesame oil
2 garlic cloves, thinly sliced

SERVES 4

Scrub the oyster shells then place one, wrapped in a clean tea towel on a firm surface with the flattest shell uppermost and the hinge pointing towards you. Gripping the oyster firmly, insert an oyster knife into the gap in the hinge and twist to snap the shells apart.

Slide the blade of the knife along the inside of the upper shell to sever the muscle that keeps the shells together. Lift the lid off the top shell, being careful not to spill any of the juices. Carefully clean away any bits of broken shell and finally run the knife under the oyster to loosen it from the shell. Repeat until all the oysters are opened, then arrange on a tray and place in the fridge until you are ready to serve.

Heat a frying pan over a medium to low heat and add the sesame seeds. Cook for 3-4 minutes, stirring regularly until they are lightly toasted. Tip out of the pan onto a plate and set aside until needed.

To serve, arrange three oysters on a bed of rock salt on each serving plate. In a bowl, mix together the soy sauce with the lime rind and juice, then spoon over the oysters. Scatter the ginger, spring onions and reserved toasted sesame seeds on top. Leave to stand for 5 minutes to allow the flavours to develop. Meanwhile, heat the sesame oil in the frying pan and sauté the garlic until it is golden and the sesame oil is nearly smoking. Drizzle over the oysters and serve immediately.

VARIATION
It is best to serve native oysters in the classic way: Put crushed ice on to the plates and then, if possible, small mounds of seaweed as it sets the oysters off so well. Arrange the opened oysters on top and have lemon wedges on hand. It is worth noting that about 15 minutes on ice is enough to chill the oyster without overdoing it.

Classic Prawn Cocktail

Prawn cocktail has enjoyed renewed popularity in recent years. Made properly with fresh ingredients, it can make an elegant yet simple starter – and it also makes an excellent sandwich filling.

20 large cooked peeled
   Dublin Bay prawns

FOR THE COCKTAIL SAUCE
6 tbsp mayonnaise (page 200)
3 tbsp tomato ketchup
1 tbsp brandy
dash of Tabasco sauce
25g/1oz wild rocket (optional)
1 Little Gem lettuce, trimmed and finely
   shredded
salt and freshly ground black pepper

SERVES 4

To make the cocktail sauce, whisk together the mayonnaise, ketchup, brandy and Tabasco sauce in a bowl. Season to taste.

To serve, lightly mix together the shredded lettuce and rocket (if using), then divide among serving glasses. Arrange the prawns on top and then drizzle over the cocktail sauce.

VARIATION
This cocktail sauce can be used with many other types of seafood such as lobster, white crab meat, poached salmon or trout. A little chopped ripe avocado is also nice mixed in with the letttuce.

Greencastle Chowder

This recipe has come from Tricia Kealy, wife of the late James Kealy from the famous Kealy's Seafood Bar in Greencastle, County Donegal. This is undoubtedly the most popular dish on their menu and Tricia doesn't like to think how many gallons of chowder they have made over the years! This delicious recipe is a fitting tribute to James.

1.2 litres/2 pints fish stock (page 204)
100g/4oz skinless salmon fillet, cubed
100g/4oz skinless haddock fillet, cubed
50g/2oz butter
1 onion, chopped
2 carrots, chopped
1 leek, chopped
3 celery sticks, chopped
1 tsp chopped fresh dill
1 tsp crushed pink peppercorns
50g/2oz plain flour
salt and freshly ground black pepper
Angostura bitters
a little milk (optional)
pouring cream and chopped fresh
    parsley, to garnish

To Serve
freshly baked baby brown scones
    (page 191)

SERVES 4-6

Bring the fish stock to a gentle simmer in a large pan and add the salmon and haddock. Cook for a couple of minutes until tender, then transfer to a plate with a slotted spoon. Set aside until needed.

Melt the butter in a separate large pan over a medium heat. Sweat the onion, carrots, leek and celery for about 10 minutes or until they are softened but not coloured. Add the dill and pink peppercorns and cook for a further 5 minutes.

Stir the flour into the vegetable mixture and cook for 5 minutes, stirring constantly. Gradually pour in the fish stock, stirring until smooth after each addition: add a dash of Angostura bitters, then bring to the boil and simmer for 15 minutes until all of the vegetables are completely tender and the liquid is slightly reduced. Season to taste.

Just before serving, a little milk can be added to thin out to desired consistency. Add the cooked salmon and haddock to the chowder and allow to warm through. Ladle into warmed bowls and garnish with a little cream and some parsley. Arrange on plates with some brown baby scones to serve.

Luxury Seafood Chowder

Ciaran Hearne from The Lobster Pot in Carne, County Wexford, says that this chowder can be prepared in advance on the day you plan to serve it, then cooled and chilled until needed. Simply warm through gently before serving. The Lobster Pot uses cubes of undyed smoked haddock, fresh salmon fillet and monkfish with cooked mussel meat, baby squid and cooked peeled prawns but you can, of course, experiment with your own selection. Don't be tempted to use oil-rich fish like smoked mackerel or smoked salmon as they are too strong and will spoil the balance of flavour.

1 onion, diced
1 courgette, diced
2 carrots, diced
300ml/½ pint dry white wine
900ml/1½ pints milk
300ml/½ pint fish stock (page 204)
1 small onion, roughly chopped
2 whole peppercorns
1 bay leaf
75g/3oz unsalted butter
75g/3oz plain flour
250g/9oz selection of prepared seafood
    (see introduction)
sea salt and freshly ground black pepper
chopped fresh flat-leaf parsley, to
    garnish

To Serve
freshly baked brown soda bread
    (page 193)

SERVES 4-6

Place the onion, courgette and carrots in a pan with the wine and, if necessary, some water, until just covered. Cover and simmer gently for about 5 minutes or until the vegetables are just tender.

Meanwhile, make a béchamel sauce base for the soup: Warm the milk and fish stock through in a pan with the onion, peppercorns and bay leaf until just coming to the boil.

In a separate large pan, melt the butter and then gradually stir in the the flour to make a roux. Remove from the heat. Strain the warmed milk and stock through a fine sieve into the roux mixture, a little at a time, stirring continuously until all the liquid is added and the mixture is completely smooth. Return the pan to a gentle heat and simmer for about 4-5 minutes until the sauce has thickened, stirring constantly.

Add the cooked vegetables and any remaining liquid into the sauce. Gently stir in the fish and seafood and cook gently on a low heat for 3-4 minutes until all the fish is just cooked and the shellfish is heated through. Ladle into warmed bowls and garnish with the parsley. Serve immediately with the brown soda bread slices.

Razor Clams with Parsley and Garlic

Terry McCoy from the Red Bank Restaurant in Skerries, County Dublin is passionate about razor clams and loves nothing better than collecting them from local beaches, where they are plentiful. This is typical of many dishes on his menu, which highlights the quality and variety of local produce available to him.

16 razor clams
50g/2oz unsalted butter
4 garlic cloves, crushed
25g/1oz flaked almonds, very finely
    chopped
10g/¼oz fresh basil leaves, finely
    chopped
15g/½oz fresh flat-leaf parsley sprigs,
    leaves stripped and finely chopped
salt and freshly ground black pepper

To Serve (optional):
freshly baked brown soda bread
    (page 193)

SERVES 4

To take the clams from their shells, gently warm the shellfish in water until the shells begin to open. Remove from the water and take all the white asparagus-shaped meat out. The spear should still be alive and pulsing. Discard any that are not. Clean the shells and place the live spears back on the shells. Arrange four shells on each heat-proof serving plate.

Preheat the grill. Melt the butter in a pan. Add the garlic, almonds, basil and parsley and sweat for 2 minutes, then drizzle over the prepared calms.

Arrange the clams under the grill for a very short time until the butter mixture cooks again. This is the critical point. If cooked too much the fish will be tough and rubbery. The reward for getting it just right is sensational. Serve at once with some brown soda bread slices, if liked.

VARIATION
This recipe also works well with large 'carpetshell' clams ('palourdes' in France).

Seared Scallops with Black Pudding and Crispy Bacon

Grainy Clonakilty black pudding from West Cork has become a favourite accompaniment for scallops in recent years, and is delicious served with bacon and classic beurre blanc sauce. But, take care when making the sauce: if allowed to become too hot or too cold the sauce will split. To find the perfect temperature, it's best to test with your finger – it should feel warm, not hot.

4 rindless streaky bacon rashers
4 slices Clonakilty black pudding
12 large scallops
2 tbsp sunflower oil
½ lemon, pips removed
25g/1oz mixed baby leaf and herb salad
2 tsp extra-virgin olive oil
salt and freshly ground black pepper

To Serve
warm beurre blanc sauce (page 201)

SERVES 4

Preheat the grill and arrange the bacon rashers and black pudding on the grill rack. Cook for 2-3 minutes, turning once until the rashers are crispy and the black pudding is cooked through.

Meanwhile, pat the scallops dry with some kitchen paper. Heat a large frying pan until it is quite hot. Add the sunflower oil, then add the scallops and sear over a high heat for 1 minute on each side until richly browned and crispy. Do this in batches if your frying pan is not very large. Transfer them to a plate, then add a squeeze of lemon juice and season to taste.

Place the baby salad leaf and herb salad in a bowl and season to taste. Drizzle over the extra-virgin olive oil, add a squeeze of lemon juice and gently toss the leaves to coat.

Arrange a mound of the dressed salad towards the back of each serving plate. Arrange the scallops around the dressed salad and pour a thin stream of the beurre blanc around the scallops. Place a piece of black pudding in the middle of each plate and top each one with a crispy rasher broken in two to serve.

Beetroot Gravadlax

This is a version of the Scandinavian alternative to smoked salmon, with the beetroot giving it a wonderful colour. It is cut by hand and traditionally served thicker than smoked salmon. The best cut for this dish is the middle of the fish.

100g/4oz coarse rock salt
75g/3oz caster sugar
1 tbsp white peppercorns, crushed
2 large beetroot, peeled and coarsely grated
2 large bunches fresh dill, fronds removed and chopped, plus extra sprigs to garnish
2 x 900g/2lb thick salmon fillets, skin on, scaled and pin bones removed

To Serve
mustard and dill sauce (page 202)

SERVES UP TO 20 AS A STARTER

To make the curing mixture; place the salt, sugar, crushed white peppercorns and beetroot in a bowl. Add half of the dill and stir to combine.

Select a large, shallow, rectangular dish, which fits the salmon comfortably, and line with clingfilm. Sprinkle a quarter of the curing mixture over the base of the dish and lay one of the salmon fillets on top, skin-side down. Sprinkle half of the curing mixture on top and cover with the other salmon, skin-side up. Sprinkle the remaining curing mixture on top and wrap the salmon fillet in the plastic film.

Weigh the salmon fillets down with some cans or weights, to help remove any excess liquid or moisture. Place in fridge for 3-4 days, turning the salmon over every 6 hours or so.

Rinse the cure off the gravadlax and pat dry with kitchen paper. Lay a large piece of clingfilm on the work surface and place one of the salmon fillets on top, skin-side down. Cover with the remaining dill and place the other salmon fillet on top, skin-side up. Wrap tightly in the clingfilm and chill for another 6 hours.

To serve, cut the gravadlax into thin slices, leaving the skin behind. Place three slices on each serving plate and add a spoonful of the sweet mustard and dill sauce to the side. Garnish with the dill fronds and serve at once.

VARIATION
For a more classic version of gravadlax omit the beetroot.

Smoked Salmon *king of smoked fish*

Along with other time-honoured methods such as salting and drying, smoking has been an essential preservation method for many foods, and especially fish, since ancient times. On a small island like Ireland, with its western coasts exposed to power of the Atlantic Ocean, the preserved harvests of the sea have always been highly valued both by the maritime communities who depend on them for their very livelihood and the wider population, who appreciate fish and seafood for its many special qualities, including the variety it brings to a diet traditionally dominated by agricultural foods. When freezing took over the job of everyday preservation the old methods became less common but, in recent years, renewed respect for artisan foods has led to a fresh appreciation of traditionally preserved foods, many of which have now found a new niche as sought-after speciality products. Dishes featured in this book highlight many of these delicious ingredients - salted ling, smoked trout and mackerel all feature, for example, and of course there are many suggestions for using the king of smoked fish, magnificent smoked salmon.

For generations smoked salmon has been revered as a particular treat - and wild Atlantic salmon, oak-smoked in the traditional way without dyes, is seen by many caring cooks as the ultimate convenience food. Although still smoked in small quantities at private fishing houses, the wild fish is no longer generally available so farmed fish is now the norm and - as with any food product - the quality varies, so it always pays to buy the best. Ireland's thriving mainstream salmon smoking industry provides a good supply of quality fish at a fair price for export and the home market, making this an accessible everyday ingredient enjoyed by a wide public. At the specialist end of the market, the renewal of interest in quality artisanal products has set the stage for a new generation of smokers, who relish everything from the careful selection of fish to a particular type of wood for the fire - in Ireland's long tradition of smoking beech, and sometimes even turf were used, but oak has always been the most common fuel. Outstanding Irish smokeries that have earned respect in Ireland and success in international competition in recent years include Sally Barnes' *Woodcock Smokery* at Castletownshend, West Cork; Frank Hederman's *Belvelly Smokehouse* at Cobh, East Cork; Anthony Cresswell's *Ummera Smokehouse* at Timoleague, West Cork; *Connemara Smokehouse* Ballyconneely, County Galway; and *The Burren Smokehouse* Lisdoonvarna, County Clare.

The Burren Smokehouse is a good example of a family enterprise producing by artisan methods an award-winning smoked salmon of individual taste, texture and flavour. Like many Irish artisan food producers, husband and wife team Peter and Birgitta Heiden-Curtin came to being specialist seafood smokers by a circuitous route. Birgitta, in her childhood on the east coast of Sweden, helped her father home-smoke eels caught in two-ended nets in the Baltic Sea; Peter had a very different background, although he had felt the call of the sea and worked first as a radio officer in the Merchant Navy, then on fishing vessels before returning to university to study science. And, by 1989, living in County Clare close to the sea, both felt drawn to explore salmon smoking.

Birgitta explains, "We travelled to many places round Ireland and Sweden to see how different smokehouses worked and what they all tasted like. Peter developed and patented a method of slow-smoking. I believe that it is what, in combination with the local microclimate of Lisdoonvarna, contributes to the very distinctive taste and texture of Burren Smokehouse salmon. It's low in salt, moist, well-smoked, but not overpowering in flavour." They source organic salmon from Clare Island in Mayo, which they say is the very best available, and use first-rate firm-fleshed farmed salmon from Donegal. Like the other smokers listed above, Peter and Birgitta have found that their products are greatly sought after by an increasingly discerning public: quality pays.

Light Bites & Salads

Smoked salmon sushi

Warm mustard tuna, avocado & watercress salad

Smoked haddock kedgeree

Baked crab hotpot

Caesar salad with sautéed prawns

Smoked salmon tagliatelle with Parmesan cream

Mussels marinières

Flash fried squid with lime & chilli dressing

Seafood laksa

Aromatic prawns

Lobster salad with lemon & dill mayonnaise

Seafood risotto

Smoked Salmon Sushi

This sushi is actually very easy to make and is far simpler to assemble than it sounds. Most large supermarkets now stock all the ingredients you'll need.

350g/12oz sushi rice
50ml/2fl oz mirin (Japanese rice wine)
6 nori sushi sheets (seaweed)
4 tsp wasabi paste
400g/14oz smoked salmon, cut into
    long thin strips
6 spring onions, trimmed
1 cucumber, cut into 6 long pieces
1 small ripe avocado, peeled, stoned and
    cut into long strips

To Serve
light soy sauce, wasabi and Japanese
    pickled ginger

SERVES 4-6

Mirin is a low-alcohol, sweet, golden wine made from glutinous rice that is essential to the Japanese cook as it adds sweetness and flavour to a variety of dishes, sauces and glazes.

Wasabi is the Japanese version of horseradish and comes from the root of an Asian plant. It comes in paste and powder form and is used to make into a green-coloured condiment that has a sharp, pungent, fiery flavour.

Nori is paper-thin sheets of dried seaweed that range in colour from dark green to dark purple to black. They have a sweet ocean taste and are generally used for wrapping sushi.

Place the rice in a sieve and rinse very well under running cold water. Drain thoroughly and put into a large pan that has a lid. Pour over 600ml/1 pint of water. Bring to the boil, then reduce the heat and allow to simmer for about 25 minutes or until all the water has been nearly absorbed. Remove from the heat, cover with a lid and leave to stand for 10 minutes.

Tip the rice onto a large flat clean tray, preferably metallic, as it will help the rice cool down more quickly. Dress the rice with the mirin, turning frequently as this helps the rice to cool, and then wave with a fan or a magazine until the rice is room temperature (this is not essential but quite authentic).

To make the sushi, take a Japanese bamboo sushi mat and place a sheet of the seaweed on top. Have a small bowl of water to hand. Dipping your fingers in the water before you touch the rice, spread the rice over half of the seaweed, taking a little rice at a time and pushing it to the edges leaving a layer about 1 cm/ $1/2$ inch thick.

Next smear a little wasabi in a line a little off centre on the side nearest to you. Follow with a layer of smoked salmon, some spring onion trimmed down to fit, a piece of cucumber and some of the avocado. Roll up the bamboo mat slowly, tucking in the closer end of the sushi to start a roll and press lightly with both hands. Remove the roll from the mat and leave to sit with the joining edges downwards. You can wrap in clingfilm and keep in a cool place for up to 1 hour until you are ready to serve. Don't place in the fridge as this dries out the rice. Repeat until all of the ingredients have been used up.

To serve, use a sharp lightly moistened knife to trim the ends, and then cut each roll into 4 pieces – you should have 24 pieces in total. Arrange on plates and serve with tiny mounds of the pickled ginger and wasabi with dipping bowls of the soy sauce.

VARIATION
You can use a wide variety of fillings in this sushi. Try smoked tuna or mackerel, for example, or fresh white crab meat; cooked peeled prawns with avocado and rocket or chives also work well.

Warm Mustard Tuna, Avocado and Watercress Salad

This salad not only looks and tastes great but it is also deceptively easy to make. Tuna cooks really quickly because it has such an open texture that the heat penetrates easily. The slices in this recipe need less than half a minute if your wok or frying pan is at the correct temperature.

350g/12oz tuna loin fillet
1 tbsp runny honey
2 tbsp wholegrain mustard
2 tbsp fresh lemon juice
1 tbsp sesame oil
1 large, firm, ripe avocado
150g/5oz watercress, well picked over
2 tbsp sesame seeds
2 tbsp extra-virgin olive oil
salt and freshly ground black pepper

To Serve
crusty bread

SERVES 4

Trim down the tuna fillet and then cut these into 1cm/½ inch slices, then slice again into strips.

Place the honey in a bowl and add the mustard, half the lemon juice and the sesame oil. Season to taste and mix until well combined, then fold in the tuna pieces. Set aside for about 5 minutes to allow the flavours to develop.

Cut the avocado in half and remove the stone, then peel the flesh and cut into thin pieces. Place in a large bowl with the watercress and season generously.

Heat a small frying pan. Add the sesame seeds and toast for a couple of minutes, tossing occasionally - you won't need any oil as the sesame seeds create enough of their own. Heat a wok or large frying pan until searing hot. Add a thin film of the olive oil, swirling it up the sides, then lay down half of the tuna slices and sear for about 20 seconds.

Carefully, turn the tuna slices over, sprinkle over the toasted sesame seeds and cook for another 10 seconds or so until tender, tossing so that each piece becomes well coated in the sesame seeds. Tip onto a plate, then wipe out the pan and repeat with the remaining ingredients. Add the remaining lemon juice and the rest of the olive oil to the pan and quickly stir together to make a dressing. Drizzle over the avocado and watercress mixture and arrange the tuna on top to serve. Have a basket of bread to hand around separately.

Smoked Haddock Kedgeree

The origins of this dish are from the glory days of the Raj in India when the leftover rice and fish from the previous evening's meal were mixed together with ghee and served for breakfast. However, it tastes so good that it is well worth making from scratch. It is much better to buy undyed smoked haddock, rather than the artificially-coloured type.

350g/12oz smoked haddock, poached
    (undyed if possible)
2 eggs
2 tbsp olive oil
½ tsp cumin seeds
1 tsp medium curry powder
225g/8oz basmati rice, well rinsed
2 tbsp sultanas
50g/2oz unsalted butter
1 small onion, finely chopped
5cm/2 inch piece fresh root ginger,
    finely grated
½ tsp ground turmeric
½ tsp tomato purée
150ml/¼ pint cream
2 tbsp chopped fresh flat-leaf parsley
salt and freshly ground black pepper

SERVES 4

Place the haddock in a small pan and cover with cold water. Bring to the boil, then reduce the heat and simmer uncovered for 3-4 minutes. Drain, reserving 3 tablespoons of the poaching liquid to add to the sauce. Allow the haddock to cool a little, then flake into bite-sized pieces; discarding any skin and bone. Boil the eggs in a small pan for 7-8 minutes (3-4 minutes longer if you like them really hard-boiled). Drain, run under cold running water, then chop.

Heat the olive oil in a large pan, then add the cumin seeds and curry powder and cook over a high heat for 1 minute, stirring. Tip in the rice and sultanas and continue to cook for another minute, stirring. Pour in 900ml/1½ pints of water and bring to the boil, then boil steadily for 10 minutes until tender.

Meanwhile make the sauce. Melt the butter in a frying pan and sauté the onion, ginger and turmeric over a medium heat for 2 minutes until softened but not browned. Stir in the tomato purée and cook for another 2 minutes, stirring. Pour in the cream and simmer for 3 minutes, then stir in the parsley and reserved poaching liquid to just heat through. Season to taste.

Use a fork to fluff up the cooked rice and then gently fold in the flaked haddock and the sauce. Divide between warmed serving bowls and garnish with the chopped hard-boiled eggs to serve.

Baked Crab Hotpot

This is a recipe for anyone who has forgotten just how gorgeous crab with cream and cheese can be – and you could pipe some mashed potatoes around the edges of the dishes if you want to go really retro... This amount will serve two as a light main course, or four as a snack or starter.

225g/8oz cooked white crab meat,
    thawed if frozen
butter, for greasing
juice of ½ lemon
1 tsp chopped fresh mixed herbs (such
    as flat-leaf parsley, chives and fennel)
300ml/½ pint béchamel sauce
    (page 199)
splash of cream
l tsp Dijon mustard
l tsp wholegrain mustard
50g/2oz red Cheddar cheese, grated
salt and freshly ground black pepper

To Serve
lightly dressed green salad (page 185)

SERVES 2-4

Preheat the oven to 180°C/350°F/Gas 4. Lightly squeeze the crab meat to remove any excess liquid and place in a bowl. Add the herbs and squeeze over enough lemon juice to taste, then lightly mix to combine. Butter two to four individual gratin dishes and divide the crab mixture among them. Season to taste.

Gently heat the béchamel sauce in a small pan and stir in the cream, then beat in the two mustards. Ladle over the crab mixture to cover completely and then sprinkle the Cheddar cheese on top. Bake for 20-25 minutes until piping hot and bubbling. Serve the dishes straight to the table with a bowl of lightly dressed green salad to hand around separately.

VARIATION

Try a selection of seafood: cooked lobster, monkfish, cod and queen scallops, for example.

Caesar Salad with Sautéed Prawns

There are those who hesitate when it comes to using anchovies in a Caesar salad. However, although they are classic, a well made Caesar salad does not need unnecessary adornment. If you really want to be correct, it is traditional for the dressing to be made with a one-minute coddled or boiled egg yolk.

2 egg yolks
1 tbsp red wine vinegar
1 tbsp fresh lemon juice
6 anchovy fillets, drained and mashed to
　　a paste
3 garlic cloves, crushed
1 tbsp Dijon mustard
½ tsp dry English mustard powder
2 tsp Worcestershire sauce
300ml/½ pint olive oil
2 large Cos lettuces or 6 Little Gem
　　lettuces, separated into leaves

To Garnish
75g/3oz freshly grated Parmesan,
　　plus extra

FOR THE SAUTÉED PRAWNS
1 tbsp olive oil
24-36 raw peeled Dublin Bay prawns,
　　veins removed

FOR THE PARMESAN CROÛTONS
175g/6oz country-style bread, crusts
　　removed and cut into 1 cm/½ inch
　　cubes
3 tbsp olive oil
25g/1oz freshly grated Parmesan
salt and freshly ground black pepper

SERVES 4-6

Preheat the oven to 150°C/300°F/Gas 2.

To make the Parmesan croûtons; place the bread cubes in a baking dish and drizzle over the olive oil, then season generously. Toss until well combined and bake for 20 minutes, then remove from the oven and scatter over the Parmesan. Return to the oven and bake for another 20-25 minutes until crisp and golden brown, stirring occasionally. These can be made in advance and stored in an airtight container.

To make the dressing, place the egg yolks in a food processor with the vinegar, lemon juice, anchovy fillets, garlic, Dijon mustard, mustard powder, Worcestershire sauce and enough pepper to suit your taste – one to one and a half teaspoons is about right. Blend together until well combined, then with the machine running, pour in the oil in a slow trickle through the feeder tube. Pour into a jug and chill until needed. Bring back up to room temperature before using, and season to taste.

To sauté the prawns, heat a large heavy-based frying pan. Add the olive oil and swirl it around the sides, then tip in the prawns and sauté for 2-3 minutes until just cooked through and tender. Season to taste.

To prepare the salad, tear the lettuce leaves into bite-sized pieces and place in a large bowl. Add enough of the dressing to just coat (not drown) the leaves, then fold in the Parmesan. Toss to combine, then transfer to wide-rimmed bowls, scatter over the Parmesan croûtons and sautéed prawns. Garnish with the extra freshly grated Parmesan to serve.

Smoked Salmon Tagliatelle with Parmesan Cream

For such a simple dish, this turns out very stylishly. There is a general rule that you should never add Parmesan to a fish-based pasta dish, but this recipe is an exception to the rule.

350g/12oz tagliatelle
225g/8oz sliced smoked salmon
4 tbsp torn fresh basil plus extra to
    garnish
300ml/½ pint double cream
6 tbsp freshly grated Parmesan
sea salt and freshly ground black pepper

SERVES 4-6

Cook the tagliatelle in a huge pan of boiling salted water – the bigger the pan the less chance of sticking - give it a stir occasionally! This can take between 8-13 minutes from boiling - check with the packet instructions, they all vary.

Cut the smoked salmon into long strips and mix with the basil. Pour the cream into a pan and bring to the boil, then boil for 1 minute until thickening; stir in 4 tablespoons of the Parmesan and season with pepper.

Drain the pasta and toss with the Parmesan cream, finally fold in the smoked salmon and basil mixture until nicely combined. Divide among warmed wide rimmed bowls and garnish with the basil to serve.

Glenbeigh Mussels 'Marinières'

This is so easy, but it is a great dish for entertaining: simple, yet impressive. This version comes from Tim Mason's seafood restaurant in Dingle, County Kerry, where head chef Seumas Macdonald cooks wonderful classics, sometimes with a modern twist. There everything depends on the fresh fish and seafood supply from the boats that day and if there's no fresh produce, they don't open.

50g/2oz butter
1 shallot, finely chopped
1.75kg/4lb fresh mussels, cleaned
150ml/¼ pint dry white wine
120ml/4fl oz cream or crème fraîche
handful chopped fresh flat-leaf parsley
freshly ground black pepper

To Serve
crusty bread

SERVES 4

Melt the butter in a large pan with a lid, add the shallot and cook over a moderate heat for 2-3 minutes until softened but not coloured.

Increase the heat, tip in the mussels and wine and cover with the lid. Allow to cook for 3–4 minutes, shaking the pan occasionally until the mussel shells have opened; discard any that do not.

Using a large slotted spoon, divide the mussels among large bowls. Whisk the cream or crème fraîche into the wine mixture and season with pepper, then pour over the mussels. Sprinkle a little of the chopped parsley over each bowl and serve with some crusty bread to mop up all those delicious juices.

VARIATION
This dish could also be made with cockles or clams instead of mussels.

Flash Fried Squid with Lime and Chilli Dressing

This is a wonderful Asian-inspired dish that is very quick to prepare. However, the squid will cook very quickly in a hot wok or frying pan; if it is cooked for too long it can become tough and chewy. Chinese five spice is an aromatic blend of spices that is now readily available in Ireland in the spice section of large supermarkets.

450g/1lb prepared squid, thawed if frozen
good pinch Chinese five spice
½ tsp freshly ground cracked black pepper
2 tsp sunflower oil
4 tbsp sweet chilli sauce
juice and finely pared rind of 2 limes
handful fresh coriander leaves, roughly chopped

SERVES 4

Cut along one side of each squid pouch and open it out flat. Score the inner side into a diamond pattern with the tip of a small, sharp knife, then cut the squid into triangles that are approximately 4cm/1½ inches. Separate the tentacles, if large. Leave to drain on kitchen paper to remove any excess liquid.

Tip the squid into a large zip-lock bag and add the Chinese five spice and pepper, then shake well to coat the squid evenly.

Heat the oil in a wok or large frying pan until very hot. Add the spiced squid and stir-fry for 30-40 seconds until just cooked through and tender. Be careful not to overcook or the squid will become rubbery.

Remove the wok from the heat. Drizzle over the sweet chilli sauce, lime juice and rind, and scatter most of the coriander on top. Quickly toss together until the squid is nicely glazed.

Arrange the squid on warmed plates and drizzle over any remaining dressing from the pan. Sprinkle with the remaining coriander and serve immediately.

Seafood Laksa

In Indonesia and Malaysia, laksa is the name of a rice noodle dish, usually with a creamy curry or tart tamarind sauce. You can now buy laksa paste in some supermarkets, but if you have the time do make your own, it makes a world of difference. This has to be the ultimate one pot noodle dish – a filling meal in itself or, served in tiny bowls, it makes a wonderful starter. Traditionally, it is garnished with laksa leaves, however, the mixture of mint and basil leaves suggested here produces an authentic flavour.

groundnut oil, for cooking

9 baby squid, cleaned and washed, cut into rings

350g/12oz monkfish fillet, skinned and cut into 5 cm/2 inch chunks

18 raw peeled Dublin Bay prawns, veins removed

1 large lemon, halved and pips removed

2 medium-hot red chillies, halved and seeded

4 garlic cloves, roughly chopped

5cm/2 inch piece fresh root ginger, peeled and roughly chopped

1 tsp ground coriander

50g/2oz bunch fresh coriander (including roots)

50ml/2fl oz sesame oil

1.2 litres/2 pints coconut milk

850ml/1½ pints fish or vegetable or chicken stock (page 204 or 203)

200g/7oz Thai rice noodles

175g/6oz sugar snap peas

50ml/2fl oz Thai fish sauce (nam pla)

To Garnish

handful fresh mint and basil leaves, thinly sliced spring onions and red chillies

SERVES 4-6

Heat a griddle pan. Brush with a little oil and then sauté the squid for 30-45 seconds on each side. Place on a plate and leave to cool, then add the monkfish and prawns. Squeeze over enough lemon juice to taste and set aside to marinate.

Heat a large pan. Place the chillies in a food processor with the garlic, ginger, ground coriander, fresh coriander and sesame oil, then blend together to a coarse paste. Add this laksa paste to the heated pan and stir-fry for 1 minute, then pour in the coconut milk and stock and bring to the boil. Simmer for 10 minutes to allow the flavours to combine and until slightly reduced, stirring occasionally.

Place the noodles in a large pan of boiling salted water and then immediately remove from the heat. Set aside for 3-4 minutes, or according to directions on the packet, then drain and refresh under cold running water. Set aside. Blanch the sugar snap peas in a small pan of boiling salted water, drain and refresh under cold running water. Set aside.

Add the fish sauce to the coconut mixture with the monkfish and prawns and stir gently for a few seconds, or until just cooked. Add the sautéed squid and stir gently for another few seconds until heated through. Divide the cooked noodles between serving bowls and scatter the sugar snap peas on top. Ladle over the coconut broth and garnish with the mint and basil leaves, spring onions and chillies to serve.

Aromatic Prawns

This clever recipe is perfect for preparing in advance to pop into the oven when you are ready to eat. The fragrant seeds and spices add a wonderful aromatic scented flavour to the prawns but will not overpower their own subtle taste. Make sure you have plenty of warm crusty bread to mop up all the delicious juices.

450g/1lb large raw peeled Dublin Bay
    prawns, veins removed
butter, for greasing
good pinch each of dill seeds, mustard
    seeds and coriander seeds
1 small onion, finely chopped
1 garlic clove, finely chopped
2 tbsp chopped fresh flat-leaf parsley
good pinch each cayenne pepper,
    ground allspice and cloves
2 tbsp white wine vinegar
4 tbsp olive oil
salt and freshly ground black pepper

To Serve
warm crusty bread

SERVES 4

Preheat the oven to 190°C/375°F/Gas 4. Place the prawns in buttered individual ovenproof dishes or one shallow casserole dish.

Heat a small frying pan and toast the dill, mustard and coriander seeds for a couple of minutes until fragrant. Tip into a mini-blender or food processor. Blend to a fine powder and then add the onion, garlic and parsley with the rest of the ground spices.

Add the wine vinegar to the mixture and then pour in the oil, in a steady trickle, until the mixture emulsifies. Pour over the prawns, place in the oven and bake for 15 minutes. Serve straight to the table with a basket of crusty bread to hand around.

Lobster Salad with Lemon and Dill Mayonnaise

This is an old favourite from Trish O'Mahony who, together with her husband Fergus, owns Mary Ann's Bar & Restaurant in Castletownshend, County Cork. This salad often makes an appearance on the daily blackboard specials in the bar; it's a dish that nobody ever seems to tire of, and which never fails to draw compliments. Freeze the leftover lobster shells and use them for lobster stock.

2 live lobsters, each about
    500g/1lb 2oz
1 small onion, sliced
1 slice lemon
1 bay leaf
2 fresh dill sprigs
handful fresh parsley stalks
few black peppercorns
120ml/4fl oz white wine
100g/4oz mixed salad leaves, such as
    chicory, rocket and lollo rosso
2 tbsp French vinaigrette (page 202)
salt and freshly ground black pepper

To Serve
lemon and dill mayonnaise (page 200)
freshly baked brown soda bread
    (page 193)

SERVES 4

To prepare the lobsters, place each one on a board and cover it with foil and a cloth. Hold firmly down with one hand and, with the point of a large knife, pierce down to the board through the cross on the centre of the head.

Put enough salted water to cover the lobsters into a large deep pan, and bring to the boil. As a guide allow at least 1 litre/1¾ pints to 1 teaspoon of salt per 500g/1lb 2oz lobster. Add the onion, lemon, bay leaf, dill sprigs, parsley, peppercorns and white wine and simmer for 5 minutes to allow the flavours to combine.

Increase the heat and when the flavoured water is boiling, add the lobsters and boil for 5 minutes for the first 500g/1lb 2oz, adding an extra 3 minutes for each extra 500g/1lb 2oz. When the lobsters are cooked, the colour changes to bright red. Transfer to a large sink or basin of iced water to cool down immediately.

When the lobsters are cool enough to handle, pull the claws from the bodies. Crack the claws and remove the meat. With a large chef's knife cut each lobster in half from the back, along the length of its body, and remove its intestinal tract, then discard. Remove the tail meat and slice it up neatly.

To serve, toss the salad leaves in the French vinaigrette, then season to taste and pile in the centre of each serving plate. Arrange the lobster meat on top and spoon a dollop of mayonnaise onto each plate. The remainder can be served in a small dish on the table along with a basket of the freshly baked brown soda bread, allowing guests to help themselves.

VARIATION
Try making this salad with only the freshest white crab meat.

Seafood Risotto

One of Italy's great simple dishes, perfect comfort food and still very fashionable at the moment. Risottos are great standby supper or lunch dishes. The secret of a good risotto is to add the stock little by little, allowing the liquid to almost disappear before adding the next ladleful.

1kg/2¼ lb mussels, cleaned
200ml/7fl oz dry white wine
600ml/1 pint fish stock (page 204)
3 tbsp extra-virgin olive oil
75g/3oz unsalted butter, chilled and
    diced
1 onion, finely chopped
2 garlic cloves, finely chopped
2.5cm/1 inch piece fresh root ginger,
    peeled and finely grated
1 red chilli, seeded and finely chopped
350g/12oz arborio rice (risotto)
pinch of saffron strands, soaked in a
    little warm water
225g/8oz small squid, cleaned and
    sliced
225g/8oz raw Dublin Bay prawns,
    peeled and veins removed
2 plum tomatoes, peeled, seeded and
    diced
2 tbsp chopped fresh flat-leaf parsley
salt and freshly ground black pepper

To Garnish
2 tbsp torn fresh basil plus extra sprigs
    to garnish

SERVES 4

Place the mussels in a pan with 50ml/2fl oz of the wine. Cover tightly and cook over a high heat for a few minutes, shaking occasionally, until all the mussels have opened - discard any that do not. Strain through a sieve. Remove the meat from mussels and reserve. Place the fish stock in a pan and strain in the mussel cooking liquor, leaving behind any grit. Bring to a gentle simmer.

Heat 2 tablespoons of the oil and 25g/1oz of the butter in a pan. Add the onion, garlic, ginger and chilli and cook for about 5 minutes until softened but not browned, stirring occasionally. Stir in the arborio rice and cook for a few minutes until nutty and perfumed. Add the remaining wine and allow to bubble away, stirring. Add a ladleful of the simmering stock and cook gently, stirring, until absorbed. Continue to add stock in this way, adding the saffron mixture after about 10 minutes - the whole process takes 20-25 minutes until the rice is tender but still 'al dente'.

Heat the remaining tablespoon of oil in a wok. Add the squid and prawns and stir-fry for 1-2 minutes, then add the tomatoes, basil, parsley and reserved mussel meat, toss together and remove from the heat. About 2 minutes before the arborio rice is cooked fold in the shellfish mixture and then fold in the remaining butter, stirring until emulsified. Ladle into wide-rimmed bowls and garnish with basil sprigs to serve.

VARIATIONS
Most seafood would be suitable for this dish: cooked lobster or crabmeat, scallops or large clams would all taste superb. Experiment with your own favourite combinations.

Arctic Charr *innovative and sustainable*

Along the Atlantic seaboard in the cold, pure water of deep glacial lakes in the West and South-West of Ireland, Arctic charr have thrived since the last ice-age.

Charr are highly prized for their meaty texture and mild, yet distinctive flavour, but elusive to anglers because of their habit of lurking at the bottom of the deep lakes. Now, thanks to an innovative aquaculture enterprise based on sustainability, eco-friendliness and harmony with its natural environment, this tasty fish is more widely available.

Bill Carty and his wife Mari Johnston were tired of commuting long distances to work 12-hour shifts, Mari as a midwife and Bill, an environmental scientist. So they made a big decision and moved to Bill's family farm in the small rural village of Cloonacool, at the foot of the Ox Mountains near Tubbercurry in County Sligo.

Their first enterprise here was mushrooms but, after some years' success, they were inspired to explore other options. Lying close to their land is Lough Talt, and it was the natural presence of Arctic charr in this lake that led them to re-develop their mushroom structures as a state-of-the-art fish farm: thus Cloonacool Arctic Charr - and Ireland's first re-circulation fish farm - was born.

In nature, charr like to lurk close to the bottom of lakes and young and old get along well together; indeed they fail to thrive unless they are able to stay in close proximity to each other, which makes them ideal candidates for farming. The aim at Cloonacool is to keep the fish as close to their natural environment as possible, and they are provided with pure spring water with nothing added except food and oxygen - no chemicals, antibiotics or colourings are used. After use in the tanks, the water is filtered through the Sligo limestone and natural reed beds before recirculation: the reeds, which are cut to the ground each winter, take up nutrients from the water - and, when this natural filtration process is complete, it is pure enough to be fed back into the tanks. (Biological filters ensure that ammonia and carbon dioxide, which accumulate naturally, are removed from the water).

Although only introduced to the market in 2006, this fish has already proved a hit with both chefs and discerning diners, who delight in the white meaty flesh with a taste that is between trout and halibut. A very healthy food, it is low in fat, rich in Omega-3 and a source of many essential nutrients, Arctic charr is available in leading restaurants, selected fishmongers and many farmers' markets.

Bill and Mari are delighted with the success of the enterprise. True, they still work long days, but they do it on the family farm and it's a source of great satisfaction.

Quick & Easy

Brill in tarragon and soured cream sauce

Grilled plaice with red onion, caper & fennel butter

Normandy style monkfish medallions

Summer seafood linguine marinara

Sichuan-style seafood stir-fry

Mackerel with citrus dressing & basil crushed potatoes

Ling in Thai curry broth

Herb & leek crusted cod

Baked salmon with smoky bacon braised cabbage & caper, garlic & dill butter

Arctic charr with lemon butter and flaked almonds

Brill in Tarragon and Soured Cream Sauce

Although not as sweetly flavoured as turbot, brill is an extremely good fish and can be good value. As with all flat fish, choose larger fish if possible, so that you get nice chunky fillets. It is quite difficult to distinguish a large brill from turbot but running your finger over the skin will soon tell you which is which as turbot have little lumps on their skin.

butter, for greasing
1.5kg/3lb large brill, filleted
175ml/6fl oz cream
1 tsp chopped fresh tarragon
2 tbsp chopped fresh flat-leaf parsley
2 tbsp fresh lemon juice
1 tsp sugar
sea salt and freshly ground black pepper

To Serve
roasted vine cherry tomatoes (page 186)

SERVES 4

Preheat the oven to 200°C/400°F/Gas 6. Butter a dish large enough to fit the brill fillets. Place the cream in a bowl and stir in the tarragon, parsley, lemon juice and sugar. Season to taste.

Arrange the brill fillets in the buttered dish and spoon over the cream mixture to cover completely. Cover with foil, place in the oven and cook for 20-25 minutes or until just cooked through and tender.

Transfer the brill fillets onto warmed plates with the roasted vine cherry tomatoes and garnish with lemon wedges to serve.

VARIATION
You can use turbot or John Dory equally successfully in this dish.

Grilled Plaice with Red Onion, Caper and Fennel Butter

From its stunning position, with views over the harbour and beach in Barna, County Galway, Michael O'Grady's charming restaurant, O'Grady's on the Pier, offers a varied seafood menu. A regular item is basic grilled fish, with the accompanying butter changed daily – very simple and straightforward, and really delicious. Alternatives to the butter given here include parsley & lemon butter and lime, chilli & coriander butter.

4 large plaice fillets
100g/4oz butter
1 small red onion, finely chopped
pinch of lemon rind
squeeze of lemon juice
a few capers
2 tbsp finely diced fresh fennel
salt and freshly ground black pepper

To Serve
braised puy lentils (page 185)
roasted Piedmont peppers (page 189)

SERVES 4

Preheat the grill.

To prepare the red onion, caper & fennel butter, place the butter in a pan with the red onion, lemon rind and juice, capers and fennel and warm together until just softening – there should still be a crunch.

Arrange the plaice fillets on a non-stick baking sheet and spoon over enough of the butter sauce to just coat. Place directly under the grill for about 4 minutes, without turning, until just cooked.

To serve, spoon the braised puy lentils onto warmed plates and arrange the roasted Piedmont peppers to the side. Warm through the remaining butter sauce and then carefully transfer the plaice fillets onto the plates, spooning the remaining butter sauce on top.

VARIATIONS
For a special occasion, use Dover sole; otherwise small brill or lemon sole would work well.

Normandy Style Monkfish

For this simple yet delicious dish, you need small monkfish tails, which have a delightful sweet flavour and are ideal cooked in this manner. A very fine purple membrane covers the monkfish fillets and, if your fishmonger has not removed it, you should take as much of it off as possible or it will cause the fillets to twist rather unattractively as they cook.

4 x 200g/7oz monkfish fillets, skinned
    and well trimmed
25g/1oz butter
1 small red apple, thinly sliced
150ml/¼ pint dry cider
150ml/¼ pint cream
salt and freshly ground black pepper

To Serve
sautéed green beans (page 187)
sautéed potatoes (page 183)

SERVES 4

Heat a large heavy-based frying pan. Melt the butter and add the fish fillets. Cook for 8-10 minutes until tender, turning them frequently to prevent them from burning. Transfer to a plate and keep warm.

Add the apple slices to the pan and sauté lightly for a couple of minutes. Add the cider and reduce by half, stirring occasionally. Add the cream and reduce until lightly thickened to a nice coating consistency.

To serve, pile the sautéed green beans onto warmed plates. Arrange the monkfish fillets on top, then spoon over the apple and cream sauce. Serve at once with a separate dish of sautéed potatoes.

Summer Seafood Linguine Marinara

The best way to treat good seafood is simply and this recipe is perfect for lazy summer evenings when you just want something light. An important part of this dish is getting the pasta just right, as the slight hardness of the pasta against the soft shellfish is what makes it so special.

1.75kg/4lb mussels, clams and cockles, cleaned
4 tbsp dry white wine
350g/12oz linguine
4 tbsp olive oil
2 garlic cloves, very finely chopped
1 red chilli, seeded and finely chopped
300ml/½ pint passata rustica (crushed tomatoes)
2 tbsp torn fresh basil
2 tbsp chopped fresh flat-leaf parsley
salt and freshly ground black pepper

SERVES 4

Place the mussels, clams and cockles in a pan with a lid and pour over the wine. Cover tightly and cook over a high heat for a few minutes, shaking the pan occasionally until all the shellfish have opened — discard any that do not. Strain through a sieve, reserving 150ml/¼ pint of the cooking liquor, and leaving behind any grit.

Meanwhile, twirl the linguine into a pan of boiling salted water; stir once and then cook for 10-12 minutes until al dente, or according to instructions on the packet.

Heat the oil in a heavy-based frying pan and add the garlic and chilli, then sauté for about 20 seconds. Pour in the passata and add the reserved cooking liquor. Bring to a gentle simmer and then stir in the cooked shellfish with basil and parsley. Season to taste and allow to just warm through.

Rinse the pasta under cold running water and drain well. Return to the pan, then pour in the seafood sauce and fold together until well combined. Divide among warmed pasta bowls and serve at once.

Sichuan-Chilli Seafood Stir-Fry

Sichuan peppercorns are the dried aromatic berries of the prickly ash tree, which is native to the Sichuan province, and they can be found in Chinese or Asian stores, or in the speciality department of good supermarkets. However, they are optional and this recipe tastes equally good with the more widely available mixed peppercorns.

1 tbsp Sichuan or mixed peppercorns
1 tbsp sea salt
350g/12oz squid, cleaned and cut into
    1 cm/½ inch slices
350g/12oz raw peeled Dublin Bay
    prawns, veins removed
225g/8oz small scallops, corals intact
1 tbsp dry sherry
2 tsp light soy sauce
2 tsp tomato purée
1 tsp sugar
2 tbsp sunflower oil
4 garlic cloves, crushed
2.5cm/1 inch fresh root ginger, peeled
    and grated
2 spring onions, finely chopped

To Serve
steamed fragrant rice (page 184)

SERVES 4-6

Heat a wok until very hot and toast the Sichuan or mixed peppercorns for a minute or two until fragrant, tossing occasionally. Tip into a spice grinder, mini-blender or mortar and pestle and add the sea salt, then grind together until coarsely cracked. Tip on to a plate and use to coat the seafood, shaking off any excess.

To make the Sichuan-style sauce, mix the sherry, soy sauce and tomato pureé in a small bowl.

Heat half of the oil in the wok until very hot. Add half the garlic, ginger and spring onions and stir-fry for 20 seconds, then tip in half of the coated seafood and continue to stir fry for 1-2 minutes until the seafood is cooked through and just tender. Repeat with the remaining ingredients.

Return all the seafood to the wok and pour over the Sichuan-style sauce. Continue to stir-fry for a minute or so until the sauce is thick and syrupy. Arrange the rice on warmed plates and spoon over the Sichuan-style seafood to serve.

Mackerel with Citrus Dressing

Mackerel is an oil-rich fish that is naturally low in saturated fat, full of vitamins and minerals, and an excellent source of essential Omega-3 fats. The body cannot make these Omega-3 fats. So, to ensure your body gets a regular supply, eat oil-rich fish, like mackerel, salmon or trout, at least once a week.

8 mackerel fillets
4 tbsp freshly squeezed orange juice
2 tbs fresh lemon juice
2 tbsp fresh lime juice
4 tbsp olive oil
1 tbsp snipped fresh chives or flat-leaf
    parsley
salt and freshly ground black pepper

To Serve
lightly dressed salad (page 185)
basil crushed new potatoes (page 180)

SERVES 4

Preheat the grill. Arrange the mackerel on the grill rack skin side up and cook under a medium heat for 5-7 minutes, or until cooked through. Some fillets of mackerel may be thicker than others, the thicker the piece of fish the longer it will take to cook. If necessary, turn once during cooking.

Whisk the orange, lemon and lime juice together in a small bowl with the olive oil and chives or parsley. Arrange the cooked mackerel fillets on warmed plates and drizzle over the citrus dressing. Add some of the lightly dressed mixed salad to the side and offer a separate dish of the basil crushed potatoes.

VARIATIONS
You can also use herring fillets in this recipe.

Ling in Thai Green Curry Broth

This is a delicious, delicately fragrant dish that has the bonus of being two meals in one — first you eat the ling and then finish with the soup. Ling is a very under-valued fish in Ireland and is much more highly prized on the continent, particularly in France. It has very white, soft flesh which parts in thick, appetising flakes when cooked.

15g/½oz bunch fresh coriander
2cm/½ inch fresh root ginger, finely
    chopped
1 lemon grass stalk, outer leaves
    removed and finely chopped
grated rind and juice of 1 lime plus extra
    lime rind to garnish
1 tbsp Thai fish sauce (nam pla) or light
    soy sauce
2 green chillies, thinly sliced plus extra to
    garnish
2 garlic cloves, crushed
2 spring onions, thinly sliced plus extra
    to garnish
1 tsp ground cumin
600ml/1 pint fish stock (page 204)
300ml/½ pint coconut milk
900g/2lb skinless ling fillet, cut into
    bite-sized cubes
salt and freshly ground black pepper

To Serve
steamed fragrant rice (page 184)

SERVES 4

Remove a good handful of the coriander leaves from the stalks for garnish and set aside. Roughly chop the remainder, including the stalks, and place in a mini-blender with the ginger, lemon grass, lime rind and juice, Thai fish sauce or soy, chillies, garlic, spring onions and cumin. Whizz to a paste or, if you don't have a mini-blender, use a pestle and mortar or chop very finely with a large knife.

Transfer the paste to a large pan with a lid and cook for 1 minute, stirring. Pour in the stock and coconut milk and bring to the boil, then reduce the heat and simmer for 5 minutes until fragrant. Season generously.

Add the ling to the pan and simmer gently for another 3-4 minutes until just tender but still holding its shape. Ladle the ling and broth into large wide rimmed serving bowls and garnish with the coriander leaves, lime rind, green chillies and spring onions. Serve at once with separate bowls of the fragrant Thai rice.

VARIATION
Replace the ling with hake, whiting, haddock, pollock or cod.

Herb and Leek Crusted Cod

This dish is a perfect example of what they do best at Cavistons Seafood Restaurant in Dun Laoghaire, County Dublin. It is simple, colourful and expertly cooked – an excellent example of just how good fish can be. Try to get your fishmonger to give you cod portions from the centre cut of the fillet so that they are nice and chunky.

2 tbsp olive oil
25g/1oz butter
2 small leeks, trimmed and finely chopped
2 tsp chopped fresh flat-leaf parsley
50g/2oz fresh white breadcrumbs
50g/2oz plain flour
4 x 200g/7oz pieces skinless cod fillet, pin bones removed
salt and freshly ground black pepper

To Serve
gratin Dauphinoise (page 183)
buttered long stem broccoli (page 191)
lemon wedges

SERVES 4

Preheat the oven to 180°C/350°F/Gas 4. Heat half of the olive oil in a pan with the butter and then sauté the leeks for 3-4 minutes until softened but not coloured. Stir in the parsley and breadcrumbs, then season to taste. Remove from the heat.

Place the flour on a flat plate and season generously, then use to coat the cod pieces, shaking off any excess. Heat the remaining oil in a large frying pan and sear the cod pieces for a minute or so on each side. Transfer to a non-stick baking tray and place in the oven for another 3 minutes.

Remove the partly-cooked cod fillets from the oven and sprinkle the breadcrumb mixture on top in an even layer. Return to the oven for another 8-10 minutes until just cooked through and tender. The time it takes will depend on the thickness of the fillets.

Transfer the herb and leek crusted cod to warmed plates with the buttered long stem broccoli. Garnish with the lemon wedges and serve with a separate dish of the gratin Dauphinoise.

Baked Salmon with Smoky Bacon, Braised Cabbage & Capers

This recipe is from Stoop Your Head Bar & Restaurant in Skerries, County Dublin, where the chef, Andy Davies, is very inventive and keen on using the best Irish produce available. This excellent dish brings together a number of traditional Irish themes and is a good example of his style.

4 x 150g/5oz skinless salmon fillets,
    pin bones removed
1 tbsp olive oil
225g/8oz butter
8 rindless smoked bacon rashers,
    thinly sliced
3 garlic cloves, finely chopped
½ head green cabbage, thick core
    removed and thinly shredded
75g/3oz capers, rinsed
juice of 1 lemon
4 fresh dill sprigs, leaves stripped and
    finely chopped
salt and freshly ground black pepper

To Serve
boiled potatoes tossed in chopped fresh
    flat-leaf parsley (page 182)

SERVES 4

Preheat the oven to 200°C/400°F/Gas 6. Place the salmon fillets on a non-stick baking sheet and season to taste, then drizzle over the olive oil. Roast for 10-12 minutes or until just tender but still very moist in the centre.

Meanwhile, melt 25g/1oz of the butter in a pan and add the bacon. Cook for 2-3 minutes until just beginning to crisp, then stir in ⅓ of the garlic and the cabbage. Cover and braise for another 2-3 minutes until the cabbage has wilted, shaking the pan every minute or so to ensure even cooking. Season with plenty of pepper and a pinch of salt.

Melt the remaining butter in a small pan and then add the rest of garlic with the capers, dill and lemon juice. Stir until nicely combined.

Divide the smoky bacon braised cabbage among bowls and place a roasted salmon fillet on each one. Drizzle over the hot butter sauce and serve with a separate dish of boiled potatoes.

VARIATION
Try using sea trout instead of salmon in this recipe.

Arctic Charr with Lemon Butter and Flaked Almonds

Arctic charr is farmed at Cloonacool, a small village at the foot of the Ox Mountains. The farm combines the best in modern, sustainable technology and ancient purity. The fish are fed with natural spring water, filtered through Sligo limestone and natural reed beds. Nothing is added to the process but food and oxygen – no chemicals, antibiotics, or colourings of any kind are used.

50g/2oz plain flour
4 x 200g/7oz Arctic charr fillets,
      skinned and bones removed
1 tbsp olive oil
50g/2oz butter
2 tbsp flaked almonds
juice of 1 lemon
2 tsp chopped fresh flat-leaf parsley
salt and freshly ground black pepper

To Serve
baby roasted fennel (page 190)

SERVES 4

Place the flour on a flat plate and season generously. Use to dust the Arctic charr fillets. Heat a large heavy-based frying pan. Add the oil and a knob of the butter and then fry the fillets for 2-3 minutes on each side until just tender. Transfer the fish to warmed plates and keep warm.

Add the remaining butter to the pan with the almonds and lemon juice. Cook for a couple of minutes, stirring constantly until the almonds are golden brown. Finally stir in the parsley and season to taste. Spoon the lemon butter and flaked almonds over the Arctic charr fillets and serve at once with the baby roasted fennel.

Clare Island Organic Salmon
nothing but the best

Thanks to unique conditions, which include siting pens in fast-moving seawater in exposed sites, low fish density and good diet, Irish farmed salmon generally has an excellent reputation internationally. And then there is Clare Island Organic Salmon, the Rolls Royce of the farmed salmon world...

Clare Island lies six kilometres off the Mayo coast in Clew Bay, on Ireland's rugged western seaboard. Weather can be severe in winter, with waves over ten metres and stormy conditions that can last for days. And it is here that Clare Island Organic Salmon, renowned for the flavour of its lean flesh and firm muscle texture, is farmed - and sustains an island community of 138 people, plus those who work for the seafarm. The idea of establishing a salmon farm here came about in 1987, when a group of islanders, keen to create employment opportunities on this off-shore island, formed a voluntary development board. As a result of this initiative, the Clare Island Salmon Farm was established in association with BIM and a Norwegian company, providing necessary funding and expertise - aquaculture is highly technical.

Ireland's Atlantic waters are classed as A1, the highest possible quality. This quality, together with the very strength of the tide and high tidal exchange, means the salmon thrive in the most exposed sea salmon farm in the world, allowing for the kind of exercise normally only found in the wild. And, exceptionally, this farm was later to be run on organic principles, so all the conditions were in place for producing fish of really outstanding quality.

The establishment of the farm encouraged qualified people to return to their native island, and also provided work for expert seafarers interested in acquiring the skills needed for salmon farming. And its success has been shared by the whole community, as it has enabled more islanders to live and bring up families on their island, supporting schools and halting a decline in population.

Although working conditions are tough, and especially hazardous in stormy weather, the enthusiastic response of leading chefs, wholesalers and exporters was proof that they were producing particularly high quality salmon. A visit from a German buyer in search of organic salmon (which he had difficulty sourcing) was the impetus for "going organic", first on a trial basis and then throughout the whole seafarm when they realised how it could make their already sought-after product even more desirable. As well as being awarded the BIM Irish Quality Organic Standard in 1996, the farm was certified organic by a number of independent international organisations in Switzerland, France and Germany. Today, much of the fish is exported worldwide and is especially highly regarded in Europe.

Clare Island is one of the largest organic salmon farms in Ireland, harvesting up to 80 tonnes every week of the year. The salmon are produced in Ireland from start to finish. Smolts or young salmon are released into eight of the most exposed cages, which have huge nets hanging underneath, allowing the fish to control their proximity to each other; natural shoaling prevents damage to their delicate skin. Here, nourished by Irish produced organic feed made from natural, GMO-free ingredients, the fish thrive. In 2730 cubic metres of water, swept by a 2-knot tidal stream every six hours, they swim the equivalent of 23,000 km in their lifetime and this exercise means they need to eat more than fish reared in a sheltered or confined environment - and it takes about 18 months before the salmon are ready for harvesting. The combination of skilled aquaculture and an ideal environment makes Clare Island Organic Salmon a premium product that is exceptionally good to eat - and highly sought after.

Family & Mid-week Meals

Creamy fish pie with prawns

Traditional fish and chips

Cheesy-grilled pollock

Tacos with crispy whiting goujons and tomato salsa

Smoked fish with wholegrain mustard sauce and poached egg

Baked cod on ratatouille with curry butter

Salmon parcels

Smoked haddock fish cakes

Warm salmon tart

Creamy Fish Pie with Prawns

This fish pie doesn't actually need to be baked in the oven as long as you use all the ingredients as soon as they are cooked. Experiment with a combination of fish, but don't be tempted to use more than half the quantity of smoked fish or the strong flavour will overpower everything else.

675g/1½lb floury potatoes, cut into
    chunks, such as Roosters
600ml /1 pint milk
300ml/½ pint cream
1 bay leaf
900g/2lb mixed firm-fleshed fish fillets,
    such as haddock and cod (fresh or
    smoked and undyed), monkfish
    and/or salmon
175g/6oz unsalted butter, plus extra for
    greasing
1 onion, finely chopped
75g/3oz plain flour
175ml/6fl oz dry white wine
2 leeks, trimmed and thinly sliced
6 tbsp chopped fresh mixed herbs, such
    as flat leaf parsley, chives and dill
350g/12oz raw peeled Dublin Bay
    prawns, veins removed
salt and freshly ground black pepper

SERVES 4-6

HINT

To serve the fish pie if made in advance,
preheat the oven to 180°C/350°F/Gas 4.
Bake for 15-20 minutes or until heated
through and the top is bubbling and
lightly golden. (If using a fan-assisted
oven bake from cold at 160°C.)

Preheat the oven to 200°C/400°F/Gas 6. Place the potatoes in a pan of boiling salted water, cover and simmer for 15-20 minutes or until tender.

Meanwhile, place milk in a small saucepan with 225ml/8fl oz of the cream and the bay leaf. Add the fish fillets and poach for 3-5 minutes or until just tender, depending on their thickness. Transfer to a plate with a fish slice and set aside until they are cool enough to handle, then flake into bite-sized chunks; discarding the skin and any bones. Strain the poaching liquid through a sieve into a jug.

Melt 50g/2oz of the butter in a large non-stick pan. Add the onion and cook gently for 4-5 minutes until softened but not coloured, stirring occasionally. Stir in the flour and cook for 2 minutes, stirring continuously. Pour in the white wine and allow to reduce, then add the reserved poaching liquid, a little at a time, whisking continuously after each addition. Reduce the heat and stir in the leeks. Simmer gently for 6-8 minutes until the leeks are softened and tender and the sauce has slightly reduced and thickened, stirring occasionally. Stir in the herbs and season to taste.

Drain the cooked potatoes and return to the pan for a couple of minutes to dry out, shaking the pan occasionally to prevent the potatoes sticking to the bottom. Mash the potatoes or pass through a potato ricer or vegetable mouli if you like a really smooth finish. Beat in the remaining butter and cream. Season to taste.

Lightly butter an ovenproof dish that is at least 30cm/12 inches in diameter and add a couple of tablespoons of the sauce. Scatter over the poached fish and the prawns, then spoon the remaining sauce on top to cover completely. Allow a light skin to form, then carefully spread over the mashed potatoes to cover completely. Smooth over with a palette knife and fluff up with a fork. Grill until completely heated through and the potato is bubbling and golden. Serve straight from the dish onto warmed plates at the table.

Traditional Fish & Chips

McDonagh's Seafood House, on Quay Street in Galway's city centre, is an informal seafood restaurant and a fish and chip takeaway combined. Both are extremely popular with locals and tourists and, once you've tasted their food, it is not difficult to understand why. The batter, which has been devised by Mary McDonagh, is a perfect combination of lightness, crispness and flavour.

8 potatoes, such as Maris Piper
2 litres/3½ pints sunflower
    or vegetable oil
4 x 175g/6oz skinless cod fillets,
    pin bones removed
salt and malt vinegar, for seasoning

FOR THE BATTER
115g/4½oz plain flour
pinch of salt
2 tbsp sunflower oil
150ml/¼ pint chilled cold water
1 egg white

To Serve
lemon wedges and pea purée (page 188)

SERVES 4

To make the chips, peel the potatoes and cut into strips no wider than 1cm/½ inch thick. Wash well in cold water to remove excess starch, then drain well. Transfer to a clean tea towel and shake until completely dry.

Preheat the oil in the fryer to 160°C/325°F. Place half of the chips in a wire basket and carefully lower into the oil. Cook until chips are soft and flexible but not browned. Remove the chips and drain well on kitchen paper. Bring the oil up to 160°C/325°F again and par-cook the remaining chips. Set the chips aside until needed.

To make the batter, sieve the flour and salt into a bowl, make a well in the centre. Pour in the oil and then gradually add the chilled cold water, carefully mixing into the flour. Whisk the egg white in a separate bowl until stiff and then fold lightly into the batter.

Preheat the oil in the fryer to 185°C/370°F. Dip the fish into the batter, then gently shake off any excess. Carefully lower into the hot oil. Deep-fry for 6-7 minutes or until the fish is cooked through and the batter is crisp and golden. Drain well on kitchen paper and keep warm in the oven - this should only be for a minute or two while you finish cooking the chips so the batter doesn't lose any of its crispness.

To finish cooking the chips, bring the oil temperature up to 175°C/345°F. Quickly cook half of the cooled chips for 1-2 minutes until they are golden brown. Drain on kitchen paper, and then cook the remainder of chips at 175°C/345°F.

Arrange the fish and chips on plates with lemon wedges and the pea purée. Season with salt and malt vinegar before serving.

Cheesy-Grilled Pollock

This has to be one of the easiest and tastiest fish dishes in the world! The topping is a wonderful store cupboard standby that's perfect for children and adults alike. The time it takes the fish will depend on the thickness of the fillet: it is important to cook it until just opaque and flaking. To check that it is cooked, gently prod the thickest part of the fish with the point of a knife and the flakes should separate easily. Red Cheddar cheese may be used for a darker coloured topping, if preferred.

2 ripe tomatoes
150g/5oz mature Cheddar cheese
4 spring onions, trimmed and finely
    chopped
4 tbsp mayonnaise
2 tbsp plain flour
4 x 150g/5oz pollock fillets, skinned and
    boned
sunflower oil, for greasing
knob unsalted butter
salt and freshly ground black pepper

To Serve
buttered green beans and peas
    (page 187)

SERVES 4

Cut the tomatoes in half and remove the seeds, then finely dice the flesh and place in a bowl. Finely dice the cheese and add to the bowl with the spring onions, then just bind with the mayonnaise. Season to taste.

Preheat the grill to high. Arrange the pollock fillets on a lightly oiled, sturdy baking sheet and season lightly, then grill for 4-6 minutes until almost tender. This will depend on the thickness of the fillet. Quickly spread the mayonnaise mixture on top and flash under the grill for another 2 minutes or until the cheese is bubbling and golden. Arrange on warmed plates with the buttered green beans and peas to serve.

VARIATION
Substitute the pollock with haddock, cod, whiting or hake.

Tacos with Crispy Whiting Goujons and Tomato Salsa

This is a great recipe for tortillas filled with deep-fried fish goujons, tomato salsa, a little soured cream and some salad. Perfect served with ice cold beer for the grown ups…

sunflower oil, for deep-frying
2 whiting, each weighing about
    350g/12oz, filleted
8 soft flour tortillas
225g/8oz Iceberg lettuce, finely
    shredded
300ml/½ pint soured cream

FOR THE BATTER
100g/4oz plain flour
50g/2oz cornflour
350ml/12 fl oz ice cold sparkling water

FOR THE SALSA
5 ripe tomatoes, skinned, seeded and
    finely chopped
1 red onion, finely chopped
2 red chillies, seeded and finely chopped
juice of 1 lime
1 tsp sugar
2 tbsp chopped fresh coriander
salt and freshly ground black pepper

SERVES 4

To make the tomato salsa, place the tomatoes in a bowl with the red onion, chillies, lime juice, sugar and coriander. Season to taste, then stir well to combine and set aside at room temperature to allow the flavours to develop.

Cut the whiting fillets into 1cm/½ inch wide strips and season generously. To make the batter, place the flour, cornflour, water and a pinch of salt into a liquidiser and blend until smooth.

Pour the sunflower oil into a pan until it is about ⅓ full and heat to 190°C/375°F or until a small piece of white bread dropped into the oil browns and rises to the surface in 1 minute. Warm the tortillas in a low oven or in the microwave, as per packet instructions.

Dip the strips of the fish into the batter, shaking off any excess and then drop them into the hot oil and cook for 4 minutes until crisp and golden brown. Lift out with a slotted spoon and drain briefly on kitchen paper.

To serve, place some lettuce down the centre of each warmed flour tortilla, top with the crispy goujons, then spoon over some tomato salsa and soured cream. Fold in the sides, roll up as tightly as you can and eat immediately.

VARIATION
Use any firm-fleshed white fish for these goujons or experiment with raw peeled Dublin Bay prawns to make scampi. Both would be delicious with a batch of homemade chips, see recipe (page 111).

Smoked Fish with Wholegrain Mustard Sauce and Poached Egg

Do make sure to get the best undyed fish possible, and don't overcook it, as this dish is so much nicer if the flakes of fish are moist – and overcooked smoked fish always has a slightly harsh aftertaste. The poached eggs can be made up to 24 hours in advance and kept in a bowl of cold water in the fridge until needed.

1 tbsp white wine vinegar
4 eggs
4 x 100g/4oz smoked fish fillets, such
    as haddock, coley or cod (preferably
    undyed)
150ml/¼ pint double cream
1 tbsp wholegrain mustard
1 tbsp clear honey
salt and freshly ground black pepper

To Serve
champ (page 181)

SERVES 4

Heat a large, shallow pan of water. Add a tablespoon of white wine vinegar and bring to the boil, then break each egg into the water where it is bubbling, reduce the heat and simmer gently for 3 minutes. Remove with a slotted spoon and plunge into a bowl of iced water. When cold, trim down any ragged ends from the cooked egg white. These will keep happily in the fridge for up to 24 hours.

Make sure all the pin bones are removed from the smoked fish. A pair of tweezers can help to remove any awkward bones. Place the fish portions in a pan and add just enough cold water to cover them. Bring to a simmer over a low heat and poach for 3-4 minutes until the fish is just cooked through and tender. Remove from the pan and keep warm.

Meanwhile, bring a large pan of salted water to the boil. Add the poached eggs and cook for 1–2 minutes to warm through. To make the wholegrain mustard sauce, place the cream in a small pan with the mustard and honey. Whisk gently to combine and season to taste, then keep warm.

To serve, place the champ on warmed plates and arrange the smoked fish on top. Using a slotted spoon, remove the poached eggs from the pan and drain briefly on kitchen paper. Place on the smoked fish and spoon over the wholegrain mustard sauce.

Baked Cod on Ratatouille with Curry Butter

Aidan MacManus of the King Sitric Fish Restaurant in Howth, County Dublin is one of the most experienced fish chefs in the country, and this dish is typical of the food served at his striking harbourside establishment. The amount of curry powder in the butter can be adjusted if the flavour proves too strong for family tastes.

50g/2oz plain flour
1 tsp hot curry powder
175g/6oz skinless cod fillets, any pin
    bones removed
2 tbsp olive oil plus extra for greasing

FOR THE CURRY BUTTER
100g/4oz butter
2 tbsp finely diced red onion
1 small garlic clove, crushed
1 tbsp hot curry powder
2 tbsp diced peeled cooking apple

FOR THE RATATOUILLE
2 tbsp olive oil
1 red onion, halved and sliced
1 garlic clove, crushed
1 red pepper, halved, seeded and diced
1 aubergine, trimmed and diced
1 courgette, trimmed and diced
225g/8oz cherry tomatoes
salt and freshly ground black pepper

SERVES 4

To make the curry butter, heat a knob of the butter and gently sauté the onion and garlic for 3-4 minutes until softened but not coloured. Stir in the curry powder and cook for another minute, then add the apple and continue to cook for another 4-5 minutes until the apple is completely tender. Remove from the heat and leave to cool completely, then beat it into the remaining butter in a small bowl and season to taste. Transfer to a square of non-stick parchment paper and roll up into a cylinder, twisting the ends to enclose. Chill for at least 2 hours until firm; it can then be sliced and used as required.

To make the ratatouille, heat the olive oil in a heavy-based frying pan and sauté the onion and garlic for 3-4 minutes until softened but not coloured. Stir in the red pepper, aubergine and courgette, cover and cook slowly for about 20 minutes, stirring occasionally. Stir in the cherry tomatoes and cook for another 5 minutes until the skins begin to split. Season to taste. This can be made in advance and gently reheated when needed.

When almost ready to serve, preheat the oven to 180°C/350°F/Gas 4. Heat a large frying pan. Place the flour and curry powder on a flat plate and season to taste. Stir to combine and then use to dust the cod fillet, shaking off any excess. Add the olive oil to the heated frying pan and then add the dusted cod fillets. Cook for 1-2 minutes each side until nicely sealed. Transfer to an oiled baking sheet. Cut the curry butter into slices and arrange on top, then roast in the oven for 6-8 minutes or until cooked through.

To serve, place a generous bed of ratatouille on each warmed plate and arrange a piece of cod on top. Add a slice of curry butter and drizzle over any remaining cooking juices.

Salmon Parcels

One of the greatest attractions of salmon is how well it adapts to different cooking methods. This is a very healthy way to cook it, but it must not be overcooked. When the parcels are opened the salmon should still be pink inside when it is served: press the flesh gently – it should give slightly, but if it is wobbly or jelly-like, it is undercooked. However, once firm, it will be overcooked, and will have lost its succulent texture.

4 x 175g/6oz skinless salmon fillet,
    pin bones removed
handful of fresh herb sprigs, choose
    from dill, parsley, coriander, marjoram
    and chives
a few green peppercorns
4 tbsp dry white wine
salt and freshly ground black pepper
lemon wedges, to garnish

To Serve
basil crushed new potatoes (page 180)

SERVES 4

Preheat the oven to 190°C/375°F/Gas 5. Using a dinner plate as a size guide, cut out four circles of non-stick parchment paper. Place a piece of salmon on each one and gently scrunch up the sides.

Scatter the herbs over the salmon portions with the peppercorns and season to taste, then drizzle a tablespoon of the wine on each one. Wrap up to enclose and arrange on a baking sheet. Bake the salmon parcels for 8-10 minutes, or until the salmon is cooked through and tender.

Open the salmon parcels and garnish each one with a lemon wedge. Serve on warmed plates with the basil crushed new potatoes, if liked.

VARIATION
Instead of salmon, try using cod, trout, lemon sole, brill or even turbot.

Smoked Haddock Fish Cakes

You could use a mixture of fish for this recipe, or you could just use one variety, and increase the quantity. Don't over-process the fish cake mixture, as it's impressive to see chunks of fish when you cut the fish cake open. If you are going to make the parsley sauce, reserve the poaching liquid from the fish and use instead of 300ml/½ pint of the milk stated in the recipe.

350g/12oz potatoes, cut into chunks
4 eggs
225g/8oz haddock fillet (in one piece)
175g/6oz smoked haddock fillet (in one piece and preferably undyed)
300ml/½ pint milk
2 fresh bay leaves
few peppercorns
100g/4oz unsalted butter
1 small onion, finely chopped
2 anchovy fillets, drained and finely chopped
2 tbsp chopped fresh flat-leaf parsley
1 tbsp chopped fresh dill
25g/1oz seasoned plain flour
100g/4oz toasted natural breadcrumbs
salt and freshly ground black pepper

To Serve
wilted spinach (page 188)
parsley sauce (page 199)

SERVES 4

Place the potatoes in a pan of boiling salted water, cover and cook for 15-20 minutes until tender. Drain and return to the pan for a couple of minutes to dry out, then mash well. Cook two of the eggs in a small pan of simmering water for 10 minutes until hard-boiled. Rinse under cold water and crack away the shell, then chop finely.

Place the fish in a large pan, add the milk, bay leaves and peppercorns. Cover and bring to a simmer, then poach for a few minutes until the fish is just tender. Transfer the fish to a plate with a fish slice and flake, discarding any skin and bones. Strain the milk into a jug – you'll need 300ml/½ pint if you want to make the parsley sauce (page 199).

Heat 25g/1oz of the butter in a frying pan and sweat the onion for about 5 minutes until softened, then add 25g/1oz of the butter and just allow to melt. Tip into a bowl and add the cooked potatoes, flaked fish, hard-boiled eggs, anchovies, parsley and dill, then mix well. Season, cover with clingfilm and chill for at least 1 hour to firm up (up to 24 hours is fine).

Shape the fish mixture into four patties and then toss in the flour. Beat the remaining two eggs in a shallow dish and add the patties turning to coat, then coat in the breadcrumbs. Arrange on a baking sheet and chill for at least 2 hours to firm up. Heat the remaining butter in a frying pan and fry the patties for 5 minutes on each side until heated through and golden brown. Arrange the spinach on plates with a fish cake on top, then pour around some of the parsley sauce to serve. The remainder of the sauce can be served in a jug so that people can help themselves.

Warm Salmon Tart

You can make the pastry case for this delicious salmon tart up to 24 hours in advance, or the raw case can be frozen for up to 3 weeks, so it is worth making more than one at a time. Alternatively, if you're short of time, use shop-bought pastry or a ready-made pastry case. Although it is lovely made with salmon, other seafood could be used instead – see variations below.

225g/8oz salmon portion
2 eggs, plus 2 egg yolks
150ml/¼ pint double cream
2 tbsp snipped fresh chives

FOR THE PASTRY
100g/4oz plain flour plus extra for
    dusting
50g/2oz unsalted butter, chilled and cut
    into cubes
1 egg
1-2 tbsp ice-cold water
salt and freshly ground black pepper

To Serve
lightly dressed fresh green salad
    (page 185)

SERVES 4-6

VARIATIONS
Replace the salmon with fresh white crab meat or raw peeled Dublin Bay prawns, or you could experiment with smoked haddock and a handful of grated mature Cheddar.

To make the pastry, place the flour, pinch of salt and the butter in a food processor and blend together briefly until the mixture resembles fine breadcrumbs, then tip into a bowl. Separate the egg and set aside the unbeaten egg white. Using a round-bladed knife, gently mix the egg yolk into the flour mixture with enough of the ice-cold water so that the pastry just comes together. Knead lightly for a few seconds on a lightly floured surface to give a smooth, firm dough. Wrap in clingfilm and chill for at least 10 minutes before rolling (or up to 1 hour is best if time allows).

Roll out the pastry on a lightly floured surface as thinly as possible and use it to line a loose-bottomed 20cm/8 inch fluted tin that is about 4cm/1½ inches deep. Chill for another 10 minutes to allow the pastry to rest.

Preheat the oven to 180°C/350°F/Gas 4. Prick the pastry base with a fork, then line with a large circle of non-stick baking paper or foil that is first crumpled up to make it easier to handle. Fill with ceramic baking beans or dried pulses and bake for about 15 minutes until the case looks 'set'.

Carefully remove the paper or foil and the beans from the 'set' pastry case and then brush the inside with the reserved unbeaten egg white to form a seal and prevent any leaks. Place back in the oven for another 5 minutes or until the base is firm to the touch and the sides are lightly coloured.

Reduce the oven temperature to 160°C/325°F/Gas 3. Cut the salmon into 2cm/¾ inch pieces, discarding all the skin and any bones. Place the eggs and yolks in a bowl and whisk to combine. Beat in the cream and chives, then season generously. Scatter the salmon in the bottom of the pastry case and season, then pour over the cream mixture. Bake for 20-25 minutes or until the tart is just set but still slightly wobbly in the centre. Leave to rest for about 5 minutes, then cut into slices and arrange on serving plates. Serve warm or cold with some fresh green salad.

Crab and Lobster
aristocrats and friends

The offer of a bite of crab or lobster is usually enough to bring a smile to any seafood lover's face - and, while lobster is undoubtedly the aristocrat of crustaceans, many would favour crab for its special flavour and relative accessibility. Lobsters are an important inshore fishery in Ireland and brown crab is fished mainly on the northwest and southwest coasts - it's the third most important Irish fishery, after mackerel and prawns. The Irish fleet has six 'vivier' vessels, which keep the crab in live holding tanks before landing and - importantly for conservation of stocks - crab are graded at sea so that those moulting (with soft shells) or in poor condition can be returned to the water.

On the east side of the Hook peninsula lies the tiny harbour of Slade, close to the Hook lighthouse. It is the home port to half-a-dozen boats, and a small group of local fishermen earn their living from the lobsters and crab that are especially plentiful in the coastal waters of the Celtic Sea, off the south Wexford coast. The rock formation in the sea off The Hook is ideal for crab and lobster, as the rocks and wrecks provide lots of the little holes and hiding places that they like.

Peter Barry is a native of the area who began fishing as a youngster during the school holidays and found he liked the life, so he's been doing it ever since. Conservation of stocks is high on the agenda. Peter Barry says, "This works for lobsters through V-notching, a system that Wexford was the first in Europe to adopt. A small notch cut into one of the tail flaps of young female lobsters creates an easily seen mark that lasts for two moults. V-notched lobsters are returned live to the sea to allow them to breed. The system is voluntary and even though the fishermen must pay a levy of 2% of their income to fund the V-notch system, it has been enthusiastically embraced by most fishermen."

Fishing for crab and lobster is hard work. Peter Barry explains just what is involved. "I have a 27-foot boat and operate 400 pots, hauling and setting about 200 each day. High season for lobster is the four summer months then, as autumn comes in, I move more towards crab which are at their best from September through to November"

"Spring is the spawning season for crab and later they have to moult their shells in order to grow. As the shell hardens they grow, and it is then that brown crab are at their best."

Peter is fortunate to be located close to his main customers, selling most of his catch to two companies who cook and vacuum-pack whole crab as well as other value-added fish and shellfish products. The lobsters are in great demand from restaurants and for export to Europe, where the excellent quality of Irish lobsters makes them a true gourmet food.

Special Occasions

Seafood fondue

Sole with lemon & hazelnut sauce

Salmon Kiev in a crust

Turbot with refrito sauce

Hot shellfish with garlic, herbs, olive oil and white wine

Black sole on the bone with lemon parsley butter

Dublin lawyer

Ray with black butter

Monkfish wrapped in Parma ham, with roasted red pepper sauce

John Dory with sauce vierge

Seafood Fondue

This is a fun way to eat seafood and a great way of using the fondue set that most of us have tucked away in the back of a cupboard. There are now some very funky fondue sets available at reasonable prices. They are mainly intended for making chocolate fondue but would work equally well with this recipe – fish is ideal for cooking at table.

12 prepared scallops
12 large raw peeled Dublin Bay prawns,
    preferably with veins removed
450g/1lb prepared squid, cut into
    bite-sized diamond pieces

FOR THE MARINADE
150ml/¼ pint olive oil
150ml/¼ pint white wine
2 garlic cloves, crushed
1 slice lemon, halved
2 bay leaves
1 fresh rosemary sprig
salt and freshly ground black pepper

To Serve
basil mayonnaise (page 200)
lemon and dill mayonnaise (page 200)
red pepper and chilli relish (page 198)

SERVES 4

To prepare the marinade, place the olive oil in a non-metallic bowl and stir in the wine, garlic, lemon, bay leaves and rosemary. Season to taste. Add the prepared seafood and set aside for 30 minutes to allow the flavours to develop.

Remove the seafood from the marinade with a slotted spoon and then thread a scallop, prawn and piece of squid onto each 10cm/4 inch wooden skewer. Arrange on a plate until needed – you should have 12 skewers in total.

Transfer the marinade to the fondue pan and simmer gently for 2 minutes, stirring frequently. Set the pan over the fondue burner at the table. Serve with the plate of prepared seafood for dipping and have bowls of the basil mayonnaise, lemon and dill mayonnaise and red pepper and chilli relish so that guests can help themselves.

VARIATION
Experiment with your favourite selection of fish and seafood for this dish. Monkfish would work extremely well as would salmon or tuna.

Sole with Lemon and Hazelnut Sauce

This recipe is the classic pairing of sole and Bénédictine liqueur, which is a brandy or cognac based herbal beverage produced in France. It is believed that Bénédictine is the oldest liqueur continuously made, having first been produced in 1510, at the Benedictine Abbey of Fécamp in Normandy. It is the same recipe that is made today, using twenty-seven plants and spices.

50g/2oz hazelnuts
75g/3oz butter
8 medium lemon sole fillets
2 tbsp Bénédictine liqueur
2 tbsp fresh lemon juice
2 tbsp chopped fresh dill
salt and freshly ground black pepper

To Serve
buttered long stemmed broccoli
    (page 191)
baked potatoes (page 182)

SERVES 4

Heat a large heavy-based frying pan. Add the hazelnuts and roast for about 5 minutes until nicely golden, stirring regularly to ensure they cook evenly. Remove from the pan and leave to cool completely, then roughly chop.

Preheat the grill to high. Melt the butter in a pan. Brush the fillets with a little of the melted butter, then season to taste. Cook under the grill for 4-6 minutes or until cooked through.

Meanwhile, add the liqueur, lemon juice and dill to the rest of the melted butter and heat gently over a low heat. Season to taste and stir in the hazelnuts.

Arrange the cooked lemon sole fillets on warmed plates with the buttered long stemmed broccoli and a baked potato. Spoon the lemon and hazelnut sauce over the lemon sole to serve.

VARIATION
You can substitute plaice, brill or black sole for the lemon sole fillets.

Salmon Kiev in a Crust

These puff pastry parcels are perfect for serving at a dinner party as there is no last minute preparation. If you want to make them up to a day in advance, dust the bottom layer of pastry with a little polenta or semolina to help prevent them from going soggy. Make sure your salmon fillets are all even-sized, at least 2.5cm/1 inch thick, otherwise the salmon is in danger of over-cooking before the pastry is ready.

100g/4oz unsalted butter, softened
2 tbsp chopped fresh tarragon
1 tbsp snipped fresh chives
1 small garlic clove, crushed
500g/1lb 2oz packet puff pastry, thawed
    if frozen (all butter, if possible)
a little plain flour, for dusting
4 x 175g/6oz salmon fillets, skinned and
    boned (each at least 2.5cm/1 inch
    thick)
50g/2oz tender young baby spinach
    leaves
good pinch freshly grated nutmeg
1 egg, beaten
salt and cracked black pepper

To Serve
steamed samphire (page 190)
hollandaise sauce (page 201)

SERVES 4

Preheat the oven to 200°C/400°F/Gas 6. Place the butter in a small bowl and beat in the tarragon with the chives, garlic, $^1/_2$ a teaspoon each pepper and salt, or to taste. Spoon on to a sheet of clingfilm or non-stick parchment paper and shape into a roll about 2.5cm/1 inch thick, then wrap tightly. Chill in the freezer for at least 10 minutes to firm up (or keep in the fridge for up to 48 hours until required, if time allows).

Cut the pastry into 8 even-sized sections and roll each one out on a lightly floured surface to a 23cm/9 inch x 15cm/6 inch rectangle, trimming down the edges as necessary. Place a salmon fillet in the centre of 4 of the pastry rectangles. Unwrap the tarragon butter, cut into slices and arrange on top, then cover with the spinach leaves. Season the spinach and add a little nutmeg.

Brush the edges of the pastry bases with a little of the beaten egg and lay a second sheet of pastry on top, pressing down to seal. Crimp the edges by gently pressing the edge of the pastry with the forefinger of one hand and between the first two fingers of the other hand. Continue all the way around the edge of the parcel, then repeat until you have 4 parcels in total. Using a sharp knife, make light slashes across each parcel but take care not to cut right through.

Place a baking sheet in the preheated oven for a few minutes. Meanwhile, brush the pastry parcels with the remaining beaten egg. Transfer to the heated baking sheet and bake for 25-30 minutes or until the pastry is cooked through and golden brown. Arrange the salmon parcels on warmed serving plates with the steamed samphire, and drizzle over the hollandaise sauce to serve.

Turbot with Refrito Sauce

Kate Cooke spent time cooking in a traditional Basque restaurant in northern Spain before opening QC's Seafood Bar & Restaurant in Cahirciveen, County Kerry with her husband, Andrew. There, fish and meat are cooked on a 'parrillia' (a Spanish charcoal grill) but you can achieve good results by using a gas grill or cast-iron frying pan. The following recipe can be used for many species of prime fish.

4 x 175g/6oz turbot fillets
120ml/4fl oz olive oil
25g/1oz unsalted butter
pinch of sea salt
4 garlic cloves, sliced
1 red chilli, seeded and split in half
4 tbsp white wine vinegar
1 tsp chopped fresh flat-leaf parsley

FOR THE BUTTER BEAN PURÉE
2 tbsp extra virgin olive oil
25g/2oz unsalted butter
1 large onion, finely chopped
2 garlic cloves, crushed
400g/14oz can butter beans, drained
    and rinsed
sea salt and freshly ground black pepper

SERVES 4

Preheat the oven to 180°C/350°F/Gas 4. To make the butter bean pureé, place the olive oil and butter in a heavy-based pan. Add the onion and garlic and cook over a gentle heat for about 10 minutes until well softened but not coloured, stirring occasionally. Stir in the butter beans and continue to cook for another few minutes until heated through and then whizz to a purée with a hand-blender. Season to taste and keep warm.

To cook the turbot, set one large or two medium cast-iron frying pans over high heat, and heat until very hot. Add a little olive oil and place the turbot in the pan, skin side up; shake the pan immediately to prevent the fish from sticking. Sear for 1 minute, then turn the fish over onto the skin side and place a small knob of butter on top, sprinkle over the sea salt and place the frying pan in the oven for about 2¹/₂-3 minutes to finish cooking .

While the fish is cooking, make the refrito sauce: Place the rest of the olive oil in a separate frying pan, add the garlic and chilli; fry gently until the garlic is golden. Place the white wine vinegar in a bowl and add the cooked garlic.

When the fish is cooked, place the fillets on heated plates. Put the frying pan back on the heat (it should have a little of the oil and juices from cooking the turbot), then add in the refrito sauce, and bring up to a very high temperature, so that the oil and vinegar blend. It will be ready when the oil and vinegar start to bubble, but be careful not to let it split. Immediately, take off the heat and add the parsley. Spoon over the turbot fillets, and divide out the lovely toasted garlic and chilli. Add some of the butter bean purée to each plate and serve.

Hot Shellfish with Garlic, Herbs, Olive Oil and White Wine

This exuberant mélange of fresh shellfish is a speciality of David Fitzgibbon from Aherne's Seafood Restaurant in Youghal, County Cork. It is simple to make if you have access to the ingredients and makes a dramatic centrepiece for a party – and of course the quantities are flexible.

675g/1 ½ lb lobster
6 prepared scallops in their half shells,
     corals intact
6 large raw peeled Dublin Bay prawns,
     veins removed
100g/4oz mussels, cleaned
100g/4oz raw native shrimps
     (preferably live)
12 crab toes
6 Pacific/Gigas oysters, opened
1 tbsp dry white wine
2 garlic cloves, crushed
1 mild red chilli, seeded and
     finely chopped
1 tbsp chopped fresh mixed herbs, such
     as flat-leaf parsley, chives and chervil
4 tbsp extra-virgin olive oil
salt and freshly ground black pepper

To Garnish
lemon wedges

SERVES 4-6

To prepare the lobster, place on a board and cover it with foil and a cloth. Hold firmly down with one hand and, with the point of a large knife, pierce down to the board through the cross on the centre of the head.

Bring a large deep pan of boiling salted water with a two-tier steamer set on top to the boil. Remove the steamer sections and add the lobster to the boiling water, then cook for 10 minutes. Lift out and set aside.

Reduce the heat to a simmer and arrange the scallops and Dublin Bay prawns in the bottom section of the steamer and put the mussels in the top section. Steam for 2 minutes, then scatter the shrimps and crab toes on top of the mussels and steam for another minute or two until all the seafood is cooked through and tender. Discard any mussels that have not opened.

Meanwhile, make the dressing: Place the wine in a small pan with the garlic, chilli, herbs and olive oil and heat gently to combine, then season to taste.

When the lobsters are cooked, the colour changes to bright red. Using a clean tea towel, pull the claws from the body. Crack the claws and then use a large chef's knife to cut each lobster in half from the back, along the length of the body; remove the intestinal tract, and discard.

Pile all of the hot shellfish on a large platter with the oysters and spoon over the warm dressing. Garnish with lemon wedges and serve at once with plenty of finger bowls for cleaning fingers.

Grilled Black Sole on the Bone

This dish from Ivans Oyster Bar & Grill in Howth, County Dublin makes use the most of a fabulous fish, known elsewhere as Dover sole. Unusually for a flat fish, black sole is best when it is two or three days old, when the flavour has intensified. Get your fishmonger to remove the coarse black skin for you.

4 medium-sized black sole
a little olive oil, for cooking
juice of ½ lemon

**FOR THE LEMON
PARSLEY BUTTER**
100g/4oz unsalted butter
squeeze of lemon juice
2 tbsp chopped fresh flat-leaf parsley
sea salt and freshly ground black pepper

To Serve
buttered mangetout
steamed new potatoes (page 182)

SERVES 4

To make the lemon parsley butter, place the butter in a mini food processor with the lemon juice and parsley. Season to taste and blend until smooth. Turn out on to a sheet of clingfilm or non-stick parchment paper and roll into a sausage shape, then twist the ends to secure. Chill for at least 2 hours until firm.

Wash the fish and dry thoroughly with kitchen paper. Heat the grill and lightly oil the grill rack. Season the fish on both sides with lemon juice and freshly ground pepper, then cook for 4-5 minutes on the skin side, depending on thickness – you will probably have to do this in batches depending on the size of your grill.

Turn the fillets carefully with a fish slice and cook the second side until the flesh is opaque and comes away easily from the bone when tested with the tip of a knife. Carefully transfer the fish to warmed plates and arrange a couple of slices of the lemon parsley butter on top of each one. Allow to melt a little and garnish with lemon wedges, then add some mangetout and steamed new potatoes to serve.

VARIATION
Good, firm medium-sized plaice or lemon sole are also excellent cooked in this manner.

Dublin Lawyer

Although nobody is absolutely sure where Dublin Lawyer got its name, wags will insist that it's probably because Dublin lawyers had a reputation for being rich and having a lot of whiskey in them!

900g/2lb live lobster
50g/2oz butter
6 tbsp cream
4 tbsp Irish whiskey
sea salt and freshly ground black pepper

SERVES 2

Plunge the lobster into boiling water for approximately 1^1/$_2$ minutes. This will kill the lobster quickly and loosen the flesh from the shell. Allow to cool, then prepare as indicated on page 22.

Rinse the shells for re-use, and keep warm. You will notice that the meat is very rare (raw); cut it into small pieces. Melt the butter in a frying pan and then stir in the cream. Simmer until reduced by half and season to taste, then tip in the lobster pieces and cook gently for 2-3 minutes.

Meanwhile, pour the whiskey into a separate small pan and quickly flambé, then pour over the lobster and cream mixture. Stir gently until just combined then, using a slotted spoon, remove the meat and place into the warmed shells. Pour any remaining sauce on top and serve immediately.

VARIATIONS

Grilled Lobster with Beurre Blanc: Pile all of the lobster meat back into the shell and season to taste, then brush with 50g/2oz of melted butter. Cook under a medium grill for about 5 minutes and offer beurre blanc on the side.

Grilled Lobster with Lemon and Parsley Butter: Pile all of the lobster meat back into the shell. In a small pan warm 50g/2oz of butter, one crushed garlic clove, a squeeze of lemon juice and a teaspoon of chopped fresh flat-leaf parsley. Season to taste and brush all over the lobster meat, reserving the remainder. Grill at medium for about 5 minutes.

Classic Lobster Thermidor: Sauté shallot in a knob of butter and then add a glug of wine and allow to bubble down completely. Stir in 6 tablespoons of cream and simmer until reduced by half, then stir in ^{1}/$_2$ a teaspoon of prepared English mustard and a squeeze of lemon juice. Finish cooking the lobster as described above; sprinkle with grated Parmesan and flash under a hot grill.

Ray with Black Butter

Ray wings have sweet pleasant flesh that slides easily off the soft ribs of the fish. When buying ray or skate, look out for really fresh fish with no smell of ammonia. This is the classic recipe for ray and the butter is not served black, but a deep nut brown. The final cooking must be done quickly in order to serve the dish piping hot.

4 pieces of ray, skinned (each weighing
    about 200g/7oz)
75g/3oz butter
1 tbsp chopped fresh flat-leaf parsley
    (optional)

FOR THE COURT BOUILLON

1 onion, sliced
2 celery sticks, sliced
1 bay leaf
few fresh parsley stalks
1 slice lemon
3 tbsp white wine vinegar
2 tsp salt
6 black peppercorns

To Serve
creamy mashed potatoes (page 180)
sautéed green beans (page 187)

SERVES 4

To make the court bouillon, pour 1.2 litres/2 pints of water into a large, shallow pan and add the onion, celery, bay leaf, parsley, lemon, vinegar, salt and peppercorns. Bring to a simmer and then cook for 5 minutes to allow the flavours to develop. Add the ray and simmer gently for 8-10 minutes.

Meanwhile, heat the butter in a small pan until golden brown. Stir in the parsley, if liked and allow to just warm through. When the ray is cooked, transfer to warmed plates with the mashed potatoes and sautéed green beans. Spoon the black butter over the ray to serve.

Monkfish with Roasted Red Pepper Sauce

This dish works extraordinarily well because the slight blandness of the monkfish contrasts very well with the sweet acidity of the roasted red pepper sauce. Fillets of monkfish are wrapped in thin slices of Parma ham, tied and roasted in the oven. For an Irish slant on this dish, try using very thinly sliced smoked bacon.

2 red peppers, halved and seeded
olive oil, for cooking
4 x 175g/6oz monkfish fillets, well
    trimmed
8 thin slices of Parma ham
knob unsalted butter
1 tsp sugar
1 tsp balsamic vinegar
100ml/3fl oz cream
sea salt and freshly ground black pepper

To Serve
wilted spinach (page 188)
roasted baby new potatoes (page 182)

SERVES 4

Preheat the oven to 200°C/400°F/Gas 6. Place the pepper halves in a small baking tin and drizzle over a little olive oil. Season lightly and then roast for 20 minutes. Transfer to a bowl and cover with clingfilm, then set aside to cool completely. This process will steam off the skins.

Wrap each monkfish fillet in 2 slices of the Parma ham and tie securely with string in two places. Melt the butter in a large, shallow ovenproof pan and add a little olive oil. Add the monkfish, seam side-up, and fry for 1-1½ minutes, until golden brown underneath. Turn over; transfer to the oven and cook for 10 minutes until the monkfish is tender and the Parma ham is crispy.

Meanwhile, remove the skins from the cooled peppers. Place in a pan with the sugar, vinegar and cream. Blend until smooth with a hand blender and season to taste, then gently warm through.

Remove the monkfish from the oven and leave to rest in a warm place for a couple of minutes, then cut into thick slices with a sharp knife. Spoon some of the roasted red pepper sauce on each warmed plate and arrange the monkfish on top. Add some wilted spinach on the side and serve with a separate bowl of roasted baby new potatoes.

John Dory with Sauce Vierge

John Dory, otherwise known as St Peter's fish, is firm-textured and well-flavoured making it suitable for almost any method of cooking. Here it is served with a sauce vierge, which is essentially an olive oil sauce that is infused with Mediterranean flavours. The simplicity and harmony of flavours allows the fish to take centre stage.

4 x 150-175g/5-6oz John Dory fillets
a little olive oil
squeeze of lemon juice

FOR THE SAUCE VIERGE
3 tbsp extra-virgin olive oil
2 garlic cloves, crushed
1 handful of flat-leaf parsley, finely
    chopped
2 tsp rinsed capers
2 anchovy fillets, drained (optional)
sea salt and freshly ground black pepper

To Serve
boiled baby new potatoes (page 182)
steamed asparagus (page 198)

SERVES 4

To make the sauce vierge, combine olive oil, garlic, parsley, capers and anchovies, if using in a food processor and blend together. (If you do not have a blender simply chop all the ingredients finely and whisk together in a bowl.) Season to taste.

Arrange the John Dory fillets in a single layer of a lightly oiled steamer and sprinkle over the lemon juice. Cook for 4-6 minutes until tender. Be careful not to undercook as, like monkfish, John Dory is best well-cooked.

Carefully remove the John Dory from the steamer. Arrange on heated plates, and then drizzle over the sauce vierge. Serve with a separate bowl of boiled baby potatoes and the steamed asparagus.

Herring and Mackerel
little treasures

Herring is one of the most traditional fish and is the fish said to have had the most influence on the economic and political history of Europe. Written records of herring fishing in Ireland can be traced back to the fifth century and archaeological evidence goes back thousands of years earlier, to the time man first settled back on the island.

As far back as history records, the size, location and abundance of herring shoals was difficult to predict. Atlantic herring, usually plentiful around the coast of Ireland, swim in enormous, fast-moving, triangular-shaped shoals, moving into shallow waters to breed, where they lay their eggs at about 120 feet – a female lays an average of 30,000 in a lifetime. Mackerel, a migratory fish, also travels in shoals. They spend the winter in deep waters and move towards the coast in Spring, to the delight of fishermen and anglers who fish off rocky shores and piers.

With the arrival of Christianity some fifteen hundred years ago, strict rules obliged the majority of the population to abstain from meat and dairy products for hundreds of days in the year. Gradually the long fasts became less onerous and all but disappeared in the mid-twentieth century. Fish was vital to the survival and health of the ordinary people and numerous methods of preserving them – salting, pickling and smoking – were developed, particularly for the readily available and inexpensive fish like mackerel, ling and herring.

From the Eighth Century onwards when the Vikings settled around the coast, established their "longphorts" and shared their seafaring skills, the catch increased enormously through fishing in deeper waters. By the late middle ages the herring was Ireland's most valuable export. Herring and mackerel can be fickle, plentiful one year and scarce the next. In Elizabethan times, valuable herring and mackerel fisheries were leased for vast amounts to foreign fishing fleets, many of whom had over-exploited their own waters.

Today herring and mackerel caught in Irish waters are valued for their taste and texture and their health-enhancing fish oil. Both are pelagic species that swim near the surface of the water and their oil, instead of being concentrated in the liver, is spread throughout the flesh. This makes them especially healthy to eat because this is the type of fat that helps keep the heart healthy.

Herring are enjoyed fresh, salted, pickled, and hot-smoked (when they are called kippers). Mackerel is one of the most beautiful fish, with striking colours and distinctive markings – a seasonal treat which has, eaten fresh from the sea, a gorgeous taste and texture. When fresh mackerel are not in season, hot-smoked mackerel is hugely popular, inexpensive and widely eaten in Ireland.

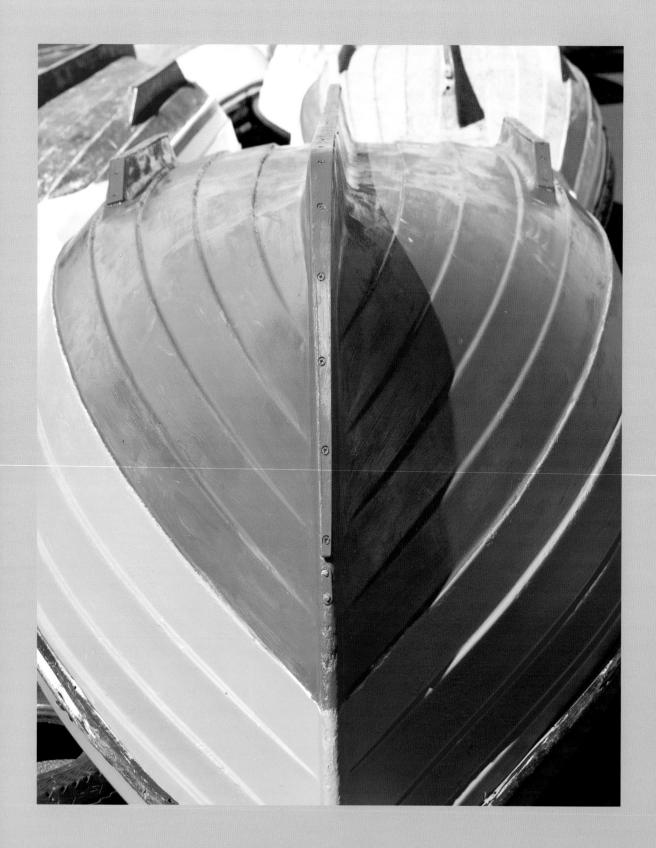

Summer Entertaining & Barbecues

Ling brandade and smoked fish platter with dillisk bread

Spicy salmon with roasted vegetable & cous cous salad

Rainbow trout with beetroot & apple preserve and warm potato salad

Grilled mackerel with three tomato salad and bruschetta

Salmon teriyaki sticks with Asian noodle salad

Mixed sandwiches and wraps platter

Wok-fried clams with spring onions, chilli and ginger butter

Whole poached salmon

Crispy hake with chorizo & black olive dressing

Salmon burger

Carrageen moss pudding with garden berry compôte

Brandade and Smoked Fish Platter

It is difficult to estimate how long you'll need to soak the salted fish but, as a rule, an hour or two should suffice if only lightly salted, or up to a day if it is very dried out. Alternatively, it is very easy to make your own. Simply put a fillet of cod or ling in a plastic bowl and completely cover with a thick layer of salt. Chill for 24 hours. After a day most of the salt will have turned into brine because so much water has been drawn out of the fish. The fish will be sufficiently preserved now to keep for up to a week.

75g/3oz beetroot gravadlax, thinly sliced
    (page 50)
75g/3oz gravadlax, thinly sliced
    (page 50)
75g/3oz smoked salmon slices
100g/4oz smoked trout fillet
100g/4oz smoked mackerel fillet,
    skin removed
50g/2oz smoked eel fillet
100g/4oz hot smoked salmon fillet
½ loaf dillisk bread, sliced (page 192)

FOR THE BRANDADE
100g/4oz salt ling, soaked (see
    introduction)
120ml/4fl oz olive oil
120ml/4fl oz cream
2 garlic cloves, peeled

To Serve
snipped fresh chives
lemon wedges

SERVES 4-6

To prepare the brandade, poach the ling in a small pan with a little water for about 10 minutes, then drain and roughly flake the flesh, removing all of the skin and bones.

Meanwhile, bring the olive oil and cream to the boil in a pan. Place the ling and the garlic in a blender or food processor and turn on. Gradually pour in the hot oil and cream mixture to build up a thick emulsion. Transfer to a serving bowl and set on a large platter. Garnish with the chives.

Arrange the beetroot gravadlax and gravadlax beside the brandade, along with the smoked salmon, smoked trout, smoked mackerel, smoked eel and hot smoked salmon. Add slices of the dillisk bread and lemon wedges before serving.

VARIATION
This brandade is made with salt ling, which is a West Cork speciality, but of course salt cod would also work well.

Spicy Salmon with Roasted Vegetable and Couscous Salad

This dish is delicious hot or cold, and works well using any combination of Mediterranean vegetables. However, it's important that the vegetables are not too crowded in the roasting tin; otherwise they'll stew rather than roast.

4 x 175g/6oz salmon fillets, skin on
2 tsp Cajun seasoning
a little olive oil

FOR THE COUSCOUS SALAD
1 red pepper, halved, seeded and cut into
　　2.5 cm/1 inch squares
1 yellow pepper, halved, seeded and cut
　　into 2.5 cm/1 inch squares
1 large courgette, chopped into
　　2.5 cm/1 inch pieces
1 small aubergine, chopped into
　　2.5 cm/1 inch pieces
1 large red onion, chopped into
　　2.5 cm/1 inch pieces
4 tbsp extra virgin olive oil
handful fresh basil leaves
175g/6oz couscous
juice of ½ lemon
salt and freshly ground black pepper

SERVES 4

Preheat the oven to 230°C/450°F/Gas 8. Heat a large roasting tin. Place the red and yellow pepper, courgette, aubergine and onion in a large bowl and drizzle over half of the oil, tossing to coat evenly, and then tip into the heated roasting tin. Season generously and roast for about 40 minutes or until the vegetables are completely tender and lightly caramelised, tossing from time to time to ensure they cook evenly. About 5 minutes before the vegetables are ready, quickly chop up the basil. Scatter over the vegetables, tossing to combine, then return to the oven to finish cooking. Set aside.

Reduce the oven temperature to 200°C/400°F/Gas 6. Place the Cajun seasoning on a flat plate and use to dust the salmon fillets, shaking off any excess. Heat an ovenproof frying pan or griddle pan. Brush with a little olive oil and sear the salmon skin side down for 30 seconds, then turn over and cook for another minute. Transfer to the oven and roast for 6-8 minutes or until tender but still very moist in the middle.

Meanwhile, finish the couscous salad. Place the couscous in a large bowl and drizzle over the remaining 2 tablespoons of the olive oil with the rest of the lemon juice, stirring to combine gently. Pour over 175ml/ 6fl oz of boiling water, then stir well, cover and leave to stand for 5 minutes before gently separating the grains with a fork. Season to taste and place in a pan to reheat gently, then fold in the roasted vegetables. Divide the roasted vegetable and couscous salad among the serving plates and then arrange the Cajun salmon fillets on top to serve.

Baked Rainbow Trout with Herbs

This is a very healthy and simple dish, perfect for a summer evening. Of course the trout could be cooked on the barbecue but this oven method really helps to keep the fish moist.

4 tsp olive oil plus extra for oiling
4 x whole rainbow trout,
    gutted and cleaned
4 tbsp white wine
2 tsp fresh lemon juice
1 tsp each chopped fresh flat-leaf
    parsley, chives, dill and basil
salt and freshly ground black pepper

To Serve
beetroot & apple preserve (page 198)
warm potato salad (page 186)

SERVES 4

Preheat the oven to 190°C/375°F/Gas 5. Lightly oil an ovenproof dish that nicely fits the size of the trout. Add the trout and then drizzle over the white wine and lemon juice. Season to taste and bake for 15-20 minutes, or until the trout are completely tender.

Remove the trout from the oven and transfer to serving plates. Mix the olive oil and herbs with the remaining juices in the dish and drizzle over the trout. Add a dollop of the beetroot and apple preserve and serve with small bowls of the warm potato salad on the side.

Grilled Mackerel with Three Tomato Salad and Bruschetta

If you plan to cook these mackerel on the barbecue try using a hinged wire rack as they make it much easier and quicker to turn the fish over during cooking and help to prevent them from sticking to the grill rack. Be careful not to overcook the mackerel, as they will dry out very quickly and become tasteless. This tomato salad is very visual and the different varieties of tomatoes each have their own individual textures and flavours.

4 whole mackerel, gutted and cleaned
8 slices country-style bread, cut on
    the diagonal
1 garlic clove, halved
olive oil, for drizzling

FOR THE THREE TOMATO SALAD
2 beef tomatoes, thinly sliced
4 ripe tomatoes, cut into wedges
100g (4oz) sunagold or baby plum
    cherry tomatoes, halved
1 shallot, thinly sliced
handful fresh basil leaves, shredded
6 tbsp balsamic and honey dressing
    (page 202)
freshly ground black pepper

SERVES 4

Preheat the grill or prepare a barbecue with medium-hot coals. Slash the mackerel through the thickest part and cook directly on a grill rack for 6-7 minutes on each side until cooked through and lightly charred.

Add the slices of bread to the grill rack for the last minute or two of cooking, turning them once. Rub with the cut side of the garlic clove and drizzle a little olive oil over each one. Keep warm.

Meanwhile, make the three tomato salad: Arrange the beef tomatoes in a single layer on the base of a large serving plate, then scatter over the tomato wedges and finish with a pile of the cherry tomatoes. Sprinkle over the shallots and basil and then drizzle the balsamic and honey dressing on top. Add a good grinding of pepper.

Serve the mackerel on plates with the bruschetta and hand the tomato salad around separately so that your guests can help themselves.

Salmon Teriyaki Sticks with Asian Noodle Salad

This is a fantastic way of cooking salmon and, as the skewers are only brushed with honey just before serving, there is no danger of them sticking to the pan and burning before the salmon is cooked. It is important to remember to soak the bamboo skewers in water if you are using the grill, otherwise, they may catch light whilst cooking.

675g/1 ½lb skinless salmon fillet, pin
    bones removed
4 tbsp dark soy sauce
2 tsp caster sugar
2 tbsp mirin (Japanese rice wine)
    or dry sherry
2 tbsp sunflower oil plus extra
    for brushing
2 tsp Dijon mustard
juice of ½ lemon
4 tbsp runny honey

To Serve
Asian noodle salad (page 187)

SERVES 4

Soak twelve bamboo skewers in cold water for at least 30 minutes. Cut the salmon into long, thin strips no more than 2.5cm/1 inch wide and about 5mm/¼ inch thick.

Place the soy sauce in a shallow non-metallic dish. Stir in the caster sugar, mirin or sherry, sunflower oil, mustard and lemon juice until well combined and the sugar has dissolved. Add the salmon strips, stirring to coat, and set aside for 15 minutes to allow the flavours to develop.

Preheat the grill or prepare a barbecue with medium-hot coals. Thread the marinated salmon onto the soaked bamboo skewers in a zig-zag fashion. Brush with a little extra oil and cook for 1-2 minutes on each side until just tender and lightly charred.

Heat the honey in a small pan or in the microwave. Remove the salmon teriyaki sticks from the grill and brush with the warm honey. Arrange three sticks on each plate with the Asian noodle salad to serve.

Mixed Sandwiches & Wraps Platter

Seafood is a great choice for a snack at lunchtime or as part of a picnic. There are now so many different types of bread available that can be served as open sandwiches – just garnish with a sprig of watercress or dill. These recipes take just minutes to make and should serve 4 (or 2 greedy adults).

CRUSTY PRAWN ROLL
Mix 350g/12oz of cooked peeled prawns with four tablespoons of cocktail sauce (page 41). Cut 4 crusty French rolls ¾ of the way through and add a little wild rocket. Top with the prawn cocktail mixture and a small diced avocado to serve.

POACHED SALMON SALAD ON BROWN SODA BREAD
Spread 8 slices of brown soda bread thinly with butter and smear with 8 tablespoons of lemon & dill mayonnaise (page 200). Add some watercress sprigs and halved cherry tomatoes and then top with 225g/8oz of poached salmon flakes (page 168). Add a sprinkling of black pepper to serve.

SMOKED SALMON AND CREAM CHEESE BAGEL
Cut 4 bagels in half and smear each bottom half with a heaped tablespoon of cream cheese. Arrange 350g/12oz of thinly sliced smoked salmon on top with some fresh watercress sprigs and add a squeeze of lemon juice to each one. Give each one a good grinding of black pepper and sandwich with the top halves of the bagels. Cut each one in half to serve.

SMOKED TROUT, MIXED LEAVES AND MUSTARD & DILL DRESSING WRAP
Spread a little mustard and dill sauce (page 202) on 4 warmed soft flour tortillas and scatter 225g/8oz of smoked trout flakes on top. Add a generous pile of mixed salad leaves to each one and drizzle over a little more of the mustard and dill dressing. Roll up and cut in half on the diagonal to serve.

CRAB WITH ROCKET AND LEMON & CHILLI MAYONNAISE
Place 4 tablespoons of mayonnaise (page 200) in a bowl and beat in ½ a teaspoon of Dijon mustard, 2 teaspoons of fresh lemon juice and a pinch of minced red chilli. Season to taste. Spread 8 slices of crusty white bread with the lemon & chilli mayonnaise. Arrange some wild rocket on half of the slices and pile 350g/12oz of fresh white crabmeat on top. Season to taste, then sandwich with the remaining slices of bread. Press down lightly, cut on the diagonal and serve.

HOT-SMOKED SALMON AND BABY SPINACH
Split 4 crusty granary rolls and smear with 3 tablespoons of mayonnaise (page 200). Arrange a handful of baby spinach leaves on the bottom halves followed by 350g/12oz of hot-smoked salmon. Add a squeeze of lemon juice and season to taste. Press the tops down lightly, then cut each one in half to serve.

SPICED SALMON WITH CURRIED MAYONNAISE

Gently fry a small finely chopped onion in a knob of butter. Add a tablespoon of mild curry paste, 1 tablespoon of honey, a glass of white wine and a handful of finely chopped ready-to-eat apricots. Simmer, uncovered for about 15 minutes until nearly all of the liquid is gone. Leave to cool, then stir in 4 tablespoons of mayonnaise (page 200) and 2 tablespoons of natural yoghurt. Roughly flake 350g/12oz of poached salmon (page 168), then fold into the apricot mixture. Spread 8 slices of brown bread with butter and divide the salmon mixture among half of them. Pile crisp shredded lettuce on top with some thinly sliced cucumber and spring onions. Cover with the remaining slices of bread and cut on the diagonal to serve.

Wok-Fried Clams with Spring Onions, Chilli & Ginger Butter

This recipe is from Martin Shanahan who owns the renowned Fishy Fishy Café in Kinsale, County Cork. He suggests using 'carpetshell' clams (or 'palourdes', as they are known in France) as they are so tender and sweet. This is a very popular way of cooking clams in the restaurant and it really does them justice.

1 kg/2½lb fresh clams, washed
60g/2¼oz butter
2 tbsp sweet chilli sauce
2 tbsp shredded fresh root ginger
2 spring onions, finely chopped
2 tbsp chopped fresh coriander plus
    extra to garnish

SERVES 4

Rinse the clams quickly in cold running water. Place in a pan with a tight fitting lid and steam for 2 minutes until opened; discard any that do not.

Heat a wok or large frying pan until almost smoking. Add the butter, sweet chilli sauce, ginger, spring onions and coriander, and use a spoon to mix together quickly.

Tip the steamed clams into the wok, and toss a couple of times, so that all the sauce coats the clams. Transfer to warmed bowls, garnish with a little more coriander and serve at once.

VARIATION
Substitute the clams with mussels and steam initially for 2-3 minutes.

Whole Poached Salmon

Salmon and celebrations tend to go hand in hand and no buffet table is complete without a magnificent dressed whole salmon as the centrepiece. This method of cooking salmon is by far the best way of producing a moist perfectly cooked fish every time. The larger the fish the more liquid required and, therefore, the longer the liquid takes to heat up and cool down again. The leftovers can be used in sandwiches (page 164).

1.8kg/4lb salmon, gutted, scaled and
    cleaned (gills removed)
150ml/¼ pint dry white wine
2 bay leaves
few slices lemon
1 small onion, sliced
few fresh parsley sprigs
few black peppercorns
1 stuffed olive, halved (optional)
salt and freshly ground black pepper
watercress sprigs and lemon wedges,
    to garnish

To Serve
lemon and dill mayonnaise (page 76)

SERVES 8

Wash the salmon well under cold running water. Remove the head
and tail if wished. To poach, place the salmon in a fish kettle. Pour
over the white wine and just enough water to cover the fish. Add the
bay leaves, lemon, onion, parsley and peppercorns. Cover the fish
kettle with a lid. Bring the liquid slowly to the boil and simmer for 2
minutes. Turn off the heat and leave the salmon (still covered) in the
liquid until it is quite cold.

When the salmon is completely cold, carefully remove the skin. Scrape
away any brown flesh to reveal the pink underneath. If the head and
tail are still on, remove the eyes, if liked, and fill the sockets with half a
stuffed olive or fresh herb sprigs. Cut a 'v' shape in the tail to neaten it.
Cover and chill for at least 30 minutes.

Place the salmon on a large serving platter and garnish with
watercress sprigs and lemon wedges to serve. Accompany with the
lemon and dill mayonnaise.

VARIATIONS
Sea trout can be used instead of the salmon.

BAKED WHOLE SALMON
Place the salmon on a large piece of buttered foil and pour over the
wine. Scatter the bay leaves, lemon, onion, parsley and peppercorns
on top. Fold the foil loosely over the fish to enclose completely.
Bake at 190°C/375°F/Gas 5 for 10 minutes per 450g/1lb until
cooked through.

Crispy Hake with Chorizo and Black Olive Dressing

Packed full of Mediterranean flavours, try this fantastic hake dish with a green salad and a nice bottle of crisp dry white wine. The key to its success is in the quality of the ingredients you use, so be sure that you seek out the best that money can buy.

2 tbsp olive oil
4 x 175g/6oz hake fillets, skin on and
    boned
25g/1oz butter
100g/4oz raw chorizo, skinned and
    cubed
100g/4oz black olives, stones removed
    (good quality)
1 tbsp chopped fresh flat-leaf parsley
good squeeze of lemon juice
salt and freshly ground black pepper

To Serve
crispy rustic potato slices with
    rosemary & garlic (page 184)

SERVES 4

Heat half of the olive oil in a large heavy-based frying pan and add the hake fillets, skin side down. Cook for a minute or two until the skin is just beginning to crisp, then add little knobs of the butter to the pan around each piece of fish and continue to cook for another minute or so until the skin is nicely crisp.

Turn the hake fillets over and cook for a further 3-4 minutes until cooked through. This will depend on the thickness of the fillets. Transfer the cooked hake fillets to a warm plate and keep warm while you make the dressing.

Add the remaining tablespoon of olive oil to the frying pan and then tip in the chorizo. Sauté for 3-4 minutes until sizzling and the chorizo has just begun to release its oil. Remove from the heat and add the olives, parsley and lemon juice. Swirl the pan around until the dressing is nicely combined and season to taste.

Arrange piles of the rustic potato slices on warmed plates and top each one with a piece of hake, skin side up. Drizzle around the chorizo and black olive dressing to serve.

VARIATIONS
This also works really well with cod or haddock.

Salmon Burger

These burgers need nothing to bind the salmon with except the mustard, but don't be tempted to blitz the salmon in the food processor as you'll lose all the wonderful texture. They would be very tasty served with spicy potato wedges (page 181) and a sun-blushed mayonnaise (see below) but they are also very nice with plain mayonnaise.

550g/1¼lb salmon fillet, skinned
    and boned
2 tbsp Dijon mustard
2 tbsp seasoned flour
1 tbsp olive oil
knob unsalted butter
4 ciabatta rolls or burger buns,
    split in half
1 small soft lettuce, separated into leaves
1 small red onion, or other mild-flavoured
    onion, separated into rings

FOR THE SUN-BLUSHED MAYONNAISE (optional)
1 tbsp sun-dried tomato paste
1 tbsp snipped fresh chives
6 tbsp mayonnaise (page 200)
salt and freshly ground black pepper

To Garnish (optional)
snipped chives
slivers of grated lemon zest

SERVES 4

Using a large sharp knife, cut away any brown bits from the salmon fillet, then finely chop. Place in a bowl, then stir in the mustard and season to taste. Divide into 4 even-sized portions, then, using slightly wetted hands, shape into patties. Dust with the seasoned flour, shaking off any excess.

Heat a griddle pan until searing hot and heat a large non-stick frying pan. Add the oil to the frying pan, then add the butter and when it stops sizzling, add the salmon burgers. Cook for 2-3 minutes on each side until lightly golden but still slightly pink in the centre.

If you would like to make the sun-blushed mayonnaise, place the sun-dried tomato paste in a small bowl with the chives and mayonnaise. Season to taste and mix until well combined.

Place the ciabatta rolls or burger buns cut-side down in the heated griddle pan, lightly toast until nicely marked and heated through. Place the bottoms on warmed serving plates. Spread over about a tablespoon of mayonnaise, then cover with some lettuce and onion rings. Place the burgers on top and finish with a little more mayonnaise. Decorate with snipped chives and grated lemon zest, if you like, and arrange on serving plates. Serve at once.

VARIATIONS
This would work well with any firm-fleshed fish such as tuna or swordfish.

Carrageen Moss Pudding with Garden Berry Compôte

This traditional carrageen pudding, set with seaweed, makes a lovely, simple dessert or can be served as part of a special breakfast; in either case the perfect accompaniment is this pretty fruit compôte, made with seasonal fruits.

5g/¼oz dried carrageen moss
1 tbsp sugar
1 small egg
900ml/1½ pints milk

FOR THE COMPÔTE
2 tbsp caster sugar
450g/1lb mixed seasonal berries, such
    as strawberries, raspberries,
blackberries, blackcurrants, blueberries,
    and loganberries
a little honey (if required)

To Decorate
fresh mint sprigs

SERVES 6

To make the carrageen pudding, soften the carrageen in a bowl of cold water; this also helps to wash it. Drain well, shaking off all of the excess water. Place the sugar and egg in a separate bowl and whisk until pale and slightly thickened. Set aside.

Bring the milk to boiling point in a small pan, then add the carrageen. Stir gently to combine, then turn down the heat to a simmer, and cook, stirring occasionally for 15 minutes. Whisk in the egg and sugar mixture.

Remove from the heat and strain into a clean bowl. Pour into six individual dishes and leave to cool completely, then place in the fridge to set for at least 30-45 minutes until nicely set.

To prepare the compôte, place the sugar in a pan with 150ml/¼ pint of water; heat gently, stirring until the sugar has dissolved, then bring to the boil. Add the berries that need longest cooking (blackcurrants, blueberries, loganberries) and cook gently for about 10 minutes, adding the softer berries towards the end. Taste, and adjust sweetness with a little honey if required. Pour into a bowl or individual serving dishes and allow to cool completely. Spoon the compôte on top of the carrageen moss pudding and decorate each one with a mint sprig to serve.

Oysters
the noble shellfish

Although they may once have been so plentiful that they were the everyday food of the ordinary people, oysters have long been associated with luxury (decadence, even!) and Irish oysters are very highly regarded internationally. Indeed, some of the most famous restaurants in Europe feature both Native and Gigas Irish oysters on their menus – and they sit easily alongside those from the River Fal in Cornwall, which are famously harvested only under sail, providing a unique and foolproof conservation measure.

Of the two species of oyster grown in Ireland, the flat native Irish oyster *(Ostrea edulis)* grows naturally on tidal sea beds and is also cultivated in managed plots. About 35 years ago, due to a decline in native stocks, Gigas *(Crassostrea gigas)*, the oval frilly-shelled Pacific oyster, was introduced and is now the main species in Ireland – cultivated by about 200 enterprises in 11 coastal counties.

Up in the rugged waters of north-west Donegal, at Tragheanna Bay, near to the town of Dungloe, Irish Premium Oysters is a family enterprise, started in1989 and now run by Edward Gallagher. Edward explains, "We have the advantage that the water in the bay – which is regularly tested and is graded class A1. Growing oysters takes patience and hard work. Some of the process is mechanised but, because it produces superior quality oysters, a lot of the work is done the hard way – by hand, working in all weathers, and with the tides. In the beginning we had setbacks; it was probably ten years before we made any money.

"Experience has taught us the best places to source our seed. We get about half from hatcheries in the UK and half from France. Water temperatures here are low so a partner in the South-East, where it is warmer, grows on the seed to about 10mm. The tiny oysters are put into 4mm plastic mesh bags and placed in the bay. It's an ideal location about 1 ½ miles wide and 2½ long. Apart from two channels it is perfectly flat – when the tide is out you have to go out a quarter of a mile to get to 30 feet of water. Even more importantly, it's fertile, with lots of seaweed and mussels, a sure sign there is plenty of natural food for the oysters."

Like mussels, oysters are not fed by the growers but take their nourishment naturally from the sea in exactly the same way as wild oysters. The bags containing the seedling oysters are turned and shaken by hand a few times during the summer. As they grow they are transferred into 9mm mesh bags and again turned regularly. When ready for harvesting the bags weigh about 15kg. The final task is to grade them by size using strict quality control methods for shape, weight and meat content. Individual oysters can weigh from 50g to over 200g.

After the long gentle growing period everything begins to move fast, the object being to get the oysters to the customers as quickly as possible. The grading machines can process 6-7,000 oysters an hour. Irish Premium Oysters are air freighted all over the world – 95% go to France, but Edward Gallagher is also supplying newly developed markets in Hong Kong, Singapore, Ukraine and Japan – the latest country to be captivated by these high quality oysters from Donegal.

Side Dishes

Creamy mashed potatoes	Roasted vine cherry tomatoes
Basil crushed new potatoes	Sautéed green beans
Champ	Asian noodle salad
Crispy potato wedges	Wilted spinach
Baked potatoes	Pea purée
Steamed/boiled new potatoes	Steamed asparagus
Gratin Dauphinoise	Roasted Piedmont peppers
Sautéed potatoes	Baby roasted fennel
Crispy rustic potato slices with rosemary & garlic	Steamed samphire
Steamed fragrant rice	Buttered purple sprouting broccoli
Braised puy lentils	Baby brown scones
Green salad	Dillisk bread
Warm potato salad	Brown soda bread

Creamy Mashed Potatoes

This is a standard mashed potato recipe which, once mastered, can be adapted for different results. Try replacing a couple of tablespoons of the milk with crème fraîche or cream for a richer version. A couple of tablespoons of chives or a good dollop of Dijon mustard can also work well, depending on what you are serving them with.

1.5kg/3lb floury potatoes, cut into even-
    sized chunks (such as Rooster)
75g/3oz butter
about 120ml/4fl oz milk
salt and freshly ground black pepper

SERVES 4-6

Place the potatoes in a large pan of salted water. Bring to the boil, cover and simmer for 15-20 minutes or until the potatoes are tender without breaking up. Drain and return to the pan over a low heat to dry out.

Mash the potatoes or pass them through a potato ricer or vegetable mouli if you want a really smooth finish. Using a wooden spoon, beat in the butter until melted and then beat in enough of the milk until you have achieved smooth, creamy mash. Season to taste and serve at once.

VARIATION
For an ultra sophisticated mash, try replacing the butter with 6 tablespoons of extra-virgin olive oil.

Basil Crushed New Potatoes

These potatoes are a kind of textured mash, so don't be tempted to make it too smooth. Pile them into a cooking ring (small metal circular mould) set on the serving plates for a really professional result.

675g/1½lb new potatoes, scraped or
    scrubbed
120ml/4fl oz extra virgin olive oil
handful fresh basil leaves
salt and freshly ground black pepper

SERVES 4-6

Place the potatoes in a large pan of boiling water and bring to the boil. Cover and simmer for 12-15 minutes until tender, then drain well.

Tip the cooked potatoes into a large bowl. Add the olive oil and with the back of a fork, gently crush each potato until it just splits. Season, and then mix carefully until all the oil has been absorbed. Finely chop the basil and stir through the potatoes, then season to taste and serve at once.

Champ

Champ is a well-loved traditional dish, especially in the north of Ireland. In the past champ would often have been served as a main dish and, in recent years, it has been enjoying a new wave of popularity as a side dish in upmarket restaurants. The flavouring in champ could be freshly chopped chives or parsley, chopped nettle tops (which would be boiled with the milk for 10 minutes), scallions (spring onions) or onions, which might be boiled with the milk like nettle tops. This basic recipe uses scallions (spring onions).

1.5kg/3lb floury potatoes
   (such as Rooster), peeled and cut
   into even-sized chunks
120ml/4fl oz milk
4 spring onions, finely chopped
75g/3oz butter
salt and freshly ground black pepper

SERVES 4-6

Place the potatoes in a large pan of cold salted water. Bring to the boil, cover and simmer for 15-20 minutes or until the potatoes are tender without breaking up. Drain and return to the pan; place over a low heat to dry out.

Just before the potatoes are ready, place the milk and spring onions in a small pan and simmer gently until the spring onions have softened in the milk, then remove from the heat.

Mash the potatoes or pass them through a potato ricer or vegetable mouli if you want a really smooth finish. Using a wooden spoon, beat in the butter until melted and then beat the milk and spring onion mixture until you have achieved a smooth, creamy mash. Season to taste and serve at once.

Crispy Potato Wedges

Try to use the best quality Cajun seasoning that you can find for this recipe, as a good balance of flavours will make all the difference to the finished dish. Whichever spices you use, don't keep them open too long in the cupboard, or they will lose all their flavour.

4 x 175g/6oz potatoes
   (about 675g/1½lb in total)
2 tbsp olive oil
½ tsp salt
1 tbsp Cajun seasoning (good quality)
salt and freshly ground black pepper

SERVES 4-6

Preheat the oven to 200°C/400°F/Gas 6. Scrub the potatoes and cut each one into 6 even-sized wedges. Place the potatoes in a pan of boiling water, return to the boil and blanch for 2-3 minutes, then quickly drain.

Put the olive oil in a large roasting tin with the salt and Cajun seasoning. Add the wedges and toss until they are all well coated in the flavoured oil, then arrange them in rows 'sitting' upright on their skins. Bake for 35-40 minutes until completely tender and lightly golden. Serve at once.

Baked Potatoes

Baked potatoes are the great standby and although they take about an hour to cook there is very little preparation to them. For the best results, choose a floury variety such as Rooster, Cara, Desirée, Maris Piper or King Edward.

4 x 200g/7oz floury potatoes, scrubbed
40g/1½oz butter

SERVES 4

Preheat the oven to 220°C/425°F/Gas 7 (fan oven 200°C) from cold. Pierce the potatoes a couple of times to prevent them from splitting, then rub them with a little salt to help give an extra crispy skin and place directly on the shelf. Bake for about 1 hour or until slightly softened when squeezed.

Boiled New Potatoes

Choose small, even-sized new potatoes for this recipe. They really should be bought (or freshly dug) in small quantities, as new potatoes that have been kept too long may look fine, but they will have an unpleasant mouldy taste when eaten.

900g/2lb small, waxy new potatoes,
    scraped or scrubbed clean
2 large fresh mint sprigs (optional)
knob of butter
sea salt

SERVES 4-6

Place the potatoes in a pan of cold water and add 1 teaspoon of salt for every pint of water. Bring to the boil and then simmer for 10 minutes.

Add one of the sprigs of mint, if using, and continue to cook for a further 2-5 minutes or until they are tender when pierced with a small sharp knife. This will all depend on the size of the potatoes.

Meanwhile, finely chop the leaves from the remaining mint sprig, if using. Drain the potatoes and return them to the pan with the butter and chopped mint. Toss briefly until the butter has melted, then serve at once.

VARIATION
New potatoes can also be steamed by simply following the instructions above. Alternatively, try roasting them in a couple of tablespoons of olive oil in a preheated oven 200°C/400°F/Gas 6 for 30-40 minutes depending on their size, until crisp and tender.

Gratin Dauphinoise

The wonderful thing about these Dauphinoise potatoes is that they can be made in advance, then reheated in individual portions on a baking sheet for about 30 minutes at the same oven temperature.

300ml/½ pint cream
300ml/½ pint milk
1 garlic clove, crushed
1.5kg/3lb potatoes, such as Maris Piper
    or King Edward
knob of butter
salt and freshly ground black pepper

SERVES 4-6

Preheat the oven 150°C/300°F/Gas 2. Place the cream and milk in a large pan with the garlic and season to taste. Peel and thinly slice the potatoes on a mandolin or using a food processor with a blade attachment.

Add the sliced potatoes to the pan and stir well to ensure that the potatoes are evenly coated. Bring to the boil, then reduce the heat and simmer for about 15 minutes until the potatoes are tender and the cream mixture has thickened slightly, stirring gently every 5 minutes or so.

Generously butter an ovenproof dish and then tip in the potato mixture, spreading them out into an even layer. Bake for about 1 hour until completely tender and lightly golden on top. Cut into portions and serve at once.

Sautéed Potatoes

These are best made with leftover potatoes or you can make from fresh by steaming 2.5cm/1 inch chunks for about 5 minutes until almost, but not quite tender. They are also good flavoured with cubes of chorizo sausage or a teaspoon of curry powder along with a couple of tablespoons of black mustard seeds, depending on your mood.

1 tbsp sunflower oil
50g/2oz butter
1.5kg/3lb leftover potatoes, peeled or
    unpeeled and cut into 2.5cm/1 inch
    cubes
sea salt

SERVES 4-6

Heat the oil in a large heavy-based pan and add the butter. Once it has stopped foaming, add the potatoes. Toss until well coated. Season to taste with salt and cook for a couple of minutes without moving to allow a crust to form. Reduce the heat and continue to sauté for another 15-20 minutes until crisp and golden brown. Serve at once.

Rustic Potato Slices with Rosemary and Garlic

These popular potato slices not only go well with a piece of pan-fried fish, but are fantastic as a side dish for a barbecue. They can be made in large quantities in trays and simply reheated as necessary.

675g/1½lb potatoes, scraped or
    scrubbed clean
1 fresh rosemary sprig, broken into tiny
    sprigs
3 garlic cloves, lightly crushed (skin still
    on)
2 tbsp olive oil
sea salt

SERVES 4-6

Preheat the oven to 200°C/400°F/Gas 6. Cut the potatoes into 5mm/¼in slices and arrange in a single layer in a roasting tin lined with non-stick parchment paper. Add the rosemary and olive oil and season generously with salt. Drizzle over the olive oil and toss until evenly coated, then roast for 15-20 minutes, or until cooked through and lightly golden. Serve at once.

Steamed Fragrant Rice

This recipe uses basmati rice, the undisputed queen of rices. It actually triples in length as it cooks and fills the house with the most heavenly scent. Of course, you can omit the spices and bay leaf if you are serving it with Asian-style dishes.

350g/12oz basmati rice
2 tbsp sunflower oil
4 whole cloves
4 green cardamom pods, cracked
5cm/2 inch piece cinnamon stick
1 bay leaf
600ml/1 pint boiling water
½ tsp salt

SERVES 4-6

Wash the rice in numerous changes of cold water until the water runs relatively clear. Cover with more cold water and leave to soak for 7 minutes, then drain well.

Heat the oil in a heavy-based pan that is approximately 20cm/8 inches in diameter, add the cloves, cardamom pods, cinnamon stick and bay leaf and cook gently over a low heat for 2-3 minutes until they start to smell aromatic.

Stir in the rice, add the boiling water and salt, then quickly bring to the boil. Stir once, cover with a tight-fitting lid, reduce the heat to low and cook over a low heat for 12 minutes, when all the water should be absorbed. Uncover, fluff up the grains with a fork and serve at once.

Braised Puy Lentils

These puy lentils are cooked with plenty of vegetable stock and have real layers of flavour. If you haven't got the time to make homemade stock, a good quality stock cube will do the trick. They can be made well in advance and reheated as needed.

2 tbsp olive oil
2 garlic cloves, finely chopped
1 mild red chilli, seeded and finely
    chopped (optional)
225g/8oz puy lentils
900ml/1½ pints vegetable stock
salt and freshly ground black pepper

SERVES 4-6

Heat the olive oil in a heavy-based pan. Stir in the garlic and chilli, if using, and sauté briefly. Add the lentils and then pour in the stock. Bring to the boil, then reduce the heat and simmer for 15-20 minutes or until tender. Drain off any excess liquid and season to taste. Use as required.

Green Salad

The secret to a good salad is to use as little dressing as possible – the leaves should barely glisten. If there's a puddle in the bottom of the salad bowl you've used too much.

1 head lettuce, such as Butterhead or
    Cos or 100g/4oz bag mixed green
    salad leaves
4-6 tbsp French vinaigrette (page 202
    or shop bought)
2 tbsp snipped fresh chives or 4 spring
    onions, finely sliced

SERVES 4-6

Break up the lettuce into individual leaves and gently tear into bite-sized pieces. Wash under cold running water and dry (use a salad spinner if you have one, as it never damages the leaves).

Turn the dried leaves into a salad bowl and drizzle over a couple of tablespoons of the dressing, then toss gently to combine and add a little more if necessary (see above). Scatter over the chives or spring onions and serve at once. Once dressed, the salad quickly begins to spoil.

VARIATION

MIXED SALAD

Add one diced avocado, a good handful of halved baby plum tomatoes and some thinly sliced red onion instead of the chives or spring onions.

Warm Potato Salad

This is perfect as part of a barbecue spread, or with a simple piece of grilled fish for a light summer supper. It is also really good served with smoked fish if you also stir in one finely chopped dill pickled cucumber and three finely diced hard-boiled eggs.

900g/2lb small, waxy new potatoes, scraped or scrubbed
2 tsp white wine vinegar
2 tbsp light olive oil
3 heaped tbsp mayonnaise
1 heaped tbsp crème fraîche
1 bunch spring onions, trimmed and thinly sliced
2 tbsp chopped fresh dill
2 tbsp chopped fresh flat-leaf parsley
salt and freshly ground black pepper

SERVES 4-6

If necessary, cut the potatoes into 2.5cm/1 inch chunks. Place in a pan of salted water, bring to the boil and cook for 12-15 minutes or until tender. This will depend on the potatoes, so keep an eye on them.

Meanwhile, in a small bowl, whisk together the white wine vinegar and the olive oil and season to taste. Drain the potatoes well, transfer to a serving bowl and gently stir in the dressing.

Stir the mayonnaise and crème fraîche together in a small bowl and stir into the potatoes, together with the spring onions, dill and parsley. Season to taste and serve at once.

Roasted Vine Cherry Tomatoes

This recipe uses cherry tomatoes still on the vine, more for presentation reasons than anything. Regular cherry tomatoes would work just as well. For a more pronounced flavour, try adding a handful of unpeeled garlic cloves.

4 cherry tomato vines, each with 5-7 tomatoes
1 tbsp olive oil
sea salt and freshly ground black pepper

SERVES 4

Preheat the oven to 200°C/400°F/Gas 6. Place the tomatoes in a small roasting tin and drizzle over the olive oil. Season to taste. Roast for 20 minutes until the tomatoes are tender and the skins have split. Serve at once.

Sautéed Green Beans

These would also be delicious with two seeded and diced vine tomatoes added to the pan with the beans, but only in the summer when tomatoes are at their best and have real flavour.

675g/1 1/2lb French green beans,
    tails removed
3 tbsp extra virgin olive oil
1 shallot, finely chopped
1 garlic clove, crushed
salt and freshly ground black pepper

SERVES 4-6

Plunge the French beans into a large pan of boiling salted water and return to the boil, then boil for a further 2 minutes until just tender. Drain and refresh under cold running water.

Return the pan to the heat with the olive oil. Add the shallot and garlic and sauté for 2-3 minutes until softened. Add the beans and continue to sauté for a minute or two until just heated through. Sprinkle in the parsley and toss until well coated. Season to taste and serve at once.

Asian Noodle Salad

This salad is packed full of fantastic textures and flavours, making it a true taste sensation. Of course you can experiment by using different types of noodles but glass noodles work very well as they soak up the sauce a treat. They also provide a great texture contrast to the crunch of the pepper, spring onions and cucumber.

225g/8oz Thai glass noodles
1 tsp sesame oil
1 large red pepper, halved, seeded and
    finely sliced
6 spring onions, finely shredded
1/2 cucumber, peeled, seeded and finely
    sliced
handful fresh coriander leaves, roughly
    chopped

FOR THE DRESSING
4 tbsp Thai fish sauce (nam pla)
4 tbsp fresh lime juice
1/2 tsp dried chilli flakes
1 1/2 tsp sugar
1 garlic clove, crushed

SERVES 4-6

Cook or soak the noodles according to packet instructions. Drain well and then toss with the sesame oil. Fold in the red pepper, spring onions and cucumber.

To make the dressing, place the Thai fish sauce in a small bowl with the lime juice, chilli flakes, sugar and garlic. Whisk until well combined and then add to the noodles, stirring until evenly combined.

If time allows, cover with clingfilm and leave for about 2 hours to absorb all the flavours. Just before serving, fold in the fresh coriander.

Wilted Spinach

This might also also be delicious with a couple of handfuls of sliced chanterelle mushrooms added with the garlic, if using; cook until tender then gently mix with the spinach.

900g/2lb fresh spinach
25g/1oz butter
1 garlic clove, crushed (optional)
pinch of freshly grated nutmeg
salt and freshly ground black pepper

SERVES 4-6

Wash the spinach and remove any large stalks, then dry well – a salad spinner is very useful if you have one. Heat a large heavy-based pan and add handfuls of the spinach, adding another as one wilts down. Cook for 1 minute, then turn into a colander and gently press out all the excess moisture.

Melt the butter in the pan and sauté the garlic for $1/2$ minute, if using, then add the drained spinach, season to taste and add a little nutmeg. Toss until heated through and then serve at once.

Pea Purée

This is a great way of serving frozen petit pois or peas. Keep a bag in the freezer and you'll soon discover that they have more flavour than most of the fresh peas that you can buy these days (often out of season). Maybe it is because they are frozen within an hour or so of being picked, whereas the fresh peas usually have to travel a long way and can take several days to reach us.

50g/2oz unsalted butter
2 small leeks, trimmed and shredded
450g/1lb frozen petit pois
    or garden peas
6 tbsp chicken stock (page 203)
pinch of sugar
salt and freshly ground black pepper

SERVES 4-6

Melt the butter in a large pan and gently sauté the leek for 3-4 minutes until tender but not coloured. Add the peas and then the chicken stock and sugar. Season to taste, then cover and simmer gently for 4-5 minutes until the peas are completely tender and most of the liquid has evaporated. Season to taste and blend to a purée with a hand-blender or in a food processor. Serve at once.

Steamed Asparagus

Of course, this is best eaten during the native asparagus season, which runs for approximately eight weeks in May and June. This is when asparagus has a full, sweet flavour and fine, tender texture. However, many supermarkets are now stocking this versatile vegetable the entire year round.

24 small asparagus spears, trimmed
knob of butter
pinch sea salt
salt and freshly ground pepper

SERVES 4-6

Cook the asparagus spears for 3-6 minutes, depending on their size in a steamer standing in 7.5 cm/3 inches of boiling water or in large pan of boiling water until just tender. Drain and toss in the butter and season with the salt. Serve at once.

VARIATION
To roast asparagus, simply preheat the oven to 200°C/400°F/Gas 6. Spread the asparagus out in a baking tin and drizzle over 2 tablespoons of olive oil, tossing until evenly coated. Sprinkle over the sea salt and roast for 6-8 minutes until tender and lightly charred. Transfer to a plate to serve.

Roasted Piedmont Peppers

Although the stalks of the peppers are not edible they do look attractive and help the peppers keep their shape. They are also delicious filled with some peeled, quartered and seeded plum tomatoes or even with a couple of anchovy fillets snipped inside before roasting.

4 large red peppers
2 tbsp olive oil plus extra for greasing
sea salt and freshly ground black pepper
fresh basil leaves, to garnish

SERVES 4-6

Preheat to 180°C/350°F/Gas 4. Cut the peppers in half and remove the seeds but leave the stalks intact. Arrange the pepper halves in a lightly oiled baking tin.

Season the pepper halves and drizzle the olive oil on top. Roast for 15-20 minutes or until the peppers are completely tender and lightly charred around the edges.

Transfer the peppers to plates and spoon over all of the cooking juices. Garnish with the basil leaves and serve warm, or at room temperature.

Baby Roasted Fennel

Unfortunately, appearance of fennel is no guide to flavour as perfect looking specimens can be poor in flavour, while battered looking fennel can be outstanding. Freshness and the soil it is grown in are the probable explanations. Its flavour is unique in vegetables and is a perfect match for fish dishes.

500g/1 ¼lb baby fennel bulbs or
    2 large fennel bulbs
2 tbsp olive oil
salt and freshly ground black pepper

SERVES 4-6

Preheat the oven to 180°C/350°F/Gas 4. Trim and cut the baby fennel bulbs into quarters and place in a large, shallow roasting tin or, if using large fennel bulbs, trim the hard round stalks at the top and discard their outer layers. Cut the remainder into thin wedges. Drizzle over the olive oil and toss to coat, then season to taste.

Place the fennel in the oven and roast until it has softened and lightly browned, stirring once or twice to ensure even cooking. Serve at once.

Steamed Samphire

The flavour of samphire is highly reminiscent of asparagus, and it is sometimes referred to as "sea asparagus". Easily recognised by its fleshy, divided aromatic leaves it has long been regarded as a delicacy in Norfolk and Lancashire. In former times, samphire was prepared as a pickle, but is now appearing as a vegetable and garnish in good restaurants. Look out for it in fishmongers and speciality shops.

450g/1lb samphire, tough stalks
    trimmed leaving the tender sprigs
25g/1oz butter
squeeze of lemon juice
freshly ground black pepper
hollandaise sauce – optional (page 201)

SERVES 4-6

Rinse the samphire in plenty of water. Bring some water to the boil in the bottom of a steamer.

Place the samphire in the top half of the steamer and steam it for 3-5 minutes until just tender and hot.

Toss the samphire in a bowl with the butter, lemon juice, and freshly ground black pepper. Serve or keep warm until ready to serve with hollandaise sauce, if liked.

Buttered Purple Sprouting Broccoli

This is a great way to ensure that broccoli is perfect every time. It can be cooked and refreshed a few hours in advance, which guarantees no more over-cooked lifeless specimens. Purple sprouting broccoli is in season in late winter and early spring, and a much more interesting vegetable than the ubiquitous calabrese.

675g/1 ½lb purple sprouting or long
    stemmed broccoli, trimmed
40g/1 ½ oz butter
salt and freshly ground black pepper

SERVES 4-6

Bring 1.75 litres/3 pints of water to the boil in a large pan with 1 tablespoon of salt. Cook the purple sprouting broccoli for 3-4 minutes, according to size. Taste, if ready, drain and plunge them into a bowl of cold water for 5 minutes to prevent further cooking. Drain again and reserve.

Heat the butter in the pan with 2 tablespoons of water until emulsified. Add the drained purple sprouting broccoli and season to taste. Sauté gently for 1 minute until just heated through. Serve at once.

Baby Brown Scones

Kealy's Seafood Bar little pub and restaurant, is on the harbour front in the rugged fishing port of Greencastle, way up in the north of Donegal. It's a small place with a big heart and, although seafood takes centre stage, the baking is exceptional. These scones are unusually light and often enhanced by a scattering of cheese on top – hard to resist.

1lb/450g plain flour plus extra for dusting
1lb/450g wheaten flour
1 tsp bread soda
1 tsp salt
725ml/1 ⅓ pints approx buttermilk (or
    use a mixture of soured cream and
    milk)
1-2 tbsp treacle, slightly warmed and
    mixed with the buttermilk
sunflower oil, for greasing
2 egg yolks mixed with 2 tbsp water
    (egg wash – optional)
50g/2oz Cheddar cheese, finely grated

MAKES 12-14

Preheat oven to 240°C/465°F/Gas 9. Sift plain flour, soda and salt into a bowl, add wheaten flour and mix well. Make a well in the centre, pour in most of the buttermilk and treacle mixture, and mix well with a wooden spoon, adding remaining liquid as needed to make a soft, moist dough. Be careful not to over mix.

Dust the worktop with flour, turn out the dough, dust the top with flour and press out evenly to a thickness of 4cm/1½ inches. Cut or stamp out individual scones with a 5cm/2 inch fluted cutter, place on an oiled and floured baking sheet and brush the tops with the egg wash and/or scatter with the grated cheese. Bake for about 12 minutes, until well risen and golden-brown. These are best eaten warm from the oven, or at least on the day of baking.

Dillisk Bread

This recipe comes from one of Ireland's most respected chefs, Gerry Galvin, who served it at the famous west of Ireland restaurant, Drimcong House, at Moycullen, County Galway which he and his wife Marie ran for many years. As well as the savoury flavour of the traditional Irish seaweed dillisk (also know as dulse), this recipe has the natural sweetness of carrot, which makes it a versatile bake that can be served as a bread or even a tea bread.

25g/1oz dried dillisk
100g/4oz butter, melted
1 large carrot, grated
4 eggs, lightly beaten
50g/2oz caster sugar
pinch of salt
250g/9oz plain white flour
½ tsp baking powder

MAKES 900G/2LB LOAF

Preheat the oven to 200°C/400°F/Gas 6. Soak the dillisk in a bowl of water for 5 minutes, then drain and pat dry with kitchen paper. Melt the butter in a small pan or in the microwave.

Brush the inside of a 900g/2lb loaf tin with a little of the melted butter. Place the remaining butter in a bowl with grated carrot, eggs, sugar, dillisk and salt. Mix lightly to combine.

Sift the flour and baking powder into a separate bowl and fold into the butter and dillisk mixture. Transfer to the prepared loaf tin and smooth the top with a palette knife. Bake for 50 minutes, or until it is springy to the touch and a skewer inserted into the centre of the loaf comes out clean. Cool in the tin before turning out, then cut into slices to serve. This bread is best eaten within two days.

Brown Soda Bread

Every day Patricia O'Mahony makes this brown bread at Mary Ann's, the O'Mahonys' famous old pub in the picturesque waterside village of Castletownshend, County Cork. The nutty flavour of this lovely moist loaf makes a particularly apt accompaniment for the delicious seafood dishes they serve in both bar and restaurant. This makes a wet mixture that is simply turned into the baking tin.

1lb/450g extra coarse wholemeal flour
    plus extra for dusting
1 tbsp bran
1 tbsp wheatgerm
1 tbsp pinhead oatmeal
1 tsp salt
1 tsp sugar
1 tsp bread soda, sieved
1 tbsp sunflower oil
1 egg, lightly beaten
450ml/3/4 pint buttermilk

MAKES ONE 900G/1LB LOAF

Preheat the oven to 230°C/450°F/Gas 8. Grease a 900g/2lb loaf tin. Place the wholemeal flour in a large bowl with the bran, wheatgerm, pinhead oatmeal, salt, sugar and bread soda, then mix lightly to combine.

Combine the oil in a jug with the egg and buttermilk. Make a well in the centre of the dry ingredients and pour in the liquid, then mix well to make a fairly wet dough. Turn into the prepared tin and bake in the oven for about an hour, removing from the tin for the last five minutes if you like a crisp crust. Cool on a wire rack and cut into slices to eat.

Dublin Bay Prawns
a little bit of history

Dubliners take pride in having a prawn named after their native city and a particularly delicious one at that. In truth, the Dublin Bay Prawn is a crustacean named *Nephrops norvegicus*, found in the Atlantic from Iceland to the Atlantic coast of Morocco and in the Mediterranean. It is the same creature as the Norwegian lobster, the French langoustine, the Italian scampi, and what Americans call a shrimp; and it is a member of the lobster family. A long slender shape, with pincer-like claws almost as long as the body, it has – like all crabs and lobsters – ten legs; pale orange in colour when alive, it only goes a beautiful coral pink when cooked. As to the origins of its common name (which is recognised far beyond these shores), *Nephrops norvegicus* has been plentiful off the east coast of Ireland for as long as anyone can remember, and the story goes that boats fishing in the Irish Sea used to shelter off the Dublin coast and, before starting to fish their way back to their home ports, the women on board would cook the fresh shellfish they had on board and sell them in the streets of Dublin as 'Dublin Bay prawns'.

Today, Ireland is one of the largest producers of prawns, and the beloved Dublin Bay Prawn is by far the most highly prized for its flavour and texture, especially when eaten whole, freshly cooked – and when the tactile pleasure of shelling them is all yours.

Anthony Kirwan, from Clogherhead in County Louth, fishes exclusively for prawns. "I come from a fishing family and started fishing in 1957 as a schoolboy, tailing prawns in my father's boat. Then we went out twice a day, morning and evening, just in the summer months and mainly in Dundalk Bay. Now, with large boats, we go out for five or six days and range far wider, trawling off the Porcupine, the Smalls, and in Area 7 off Cornwall. The largest Irish boats fish off the west coast. There are five boats in my immediate family and I own three. These days my two sons, Tony and Barry, go to sea with a crew of six and the skipper. Each trawl covers about 22 miles and, travelling at 2-3 miles an hour, takes about four hours. Trawling is done when the tides are slack and the prawns come out of their burrows to feed."

Prawns live in burrows at depths between 10 and 500 metres, only leaving to mate and to feed. Prawn fishermen work antisocial hours because prawns tend to emerge at dawn, twilight, or on nights with a full moon. Like all crustaceans they carry their skeleton on the outside, supporting the soft tissue of their flesh within; this 'exoskeleton' doesn't grow as the body grows and is shed, or moulted, at regular intervals. In Irish waters prawns breed every year, mating in early summer; females carry around a clump of fertilised green eggs under their tail until they hatch the following spring. Fortunately for the next generation, females tend to keep to the burrow and are rarely caught in trawls.

Anthony adds, "Dublin Bay Prawns are in great demand for their excellent quality and texture. Using modern ice-making machines prawns keep well for several days and, while the smaller ones are tailed at sea (a labour-intensive process) and go to a scampi factory, larger, whole prawns go to local fish processors."

Sauces, Dressings, Stocks & Preserves

Red pepper & chilli relish

Beetroot & apple preserve

Béchamel sauce (with variations)

Mayonnaise (with variations)

Sweet mustard dressing

Hollandaise sauce

Beurre blanc

Mustard & dill sauce

French vinaigrette

Vegetable stock

Chicken stock

Fish stock

Red Pepper & Chilli Relish

The natural sweetness of the red onion gives this a wonderful mellow flavour. This relish is great with barbecued fish or crab cakes (page 29), or the salmon burger (page 172). It will keep in the fridge for up to a week.

2 tbsp olive oil
1 red pepper, halved seeded and
    chopped
2 red onions, chopped
3 red chillies, seeded
2 tsp sugar
2 tomatoes, skinned and chopped

MAKES ABOUT 300ML/^{1}/$_2$ PINT

Heat the olive oil in a heavy-based pan. Add the red pepper, red onions and chillies and cook over a low heat for 30 minutes until the vegetables are completely tender but not coloured, stirring regularly.

Sprinkle the sugar over the vegetable mixture and add the tomatoes, then simmer for another 10 minutes until slightly reduced and thickened. Leave to cool and then blend in a food processor or with a hand-blender, to make a thick purée. Season to taste and place in a sterilised jar. Store in the fridge and use as required.

Beetroot & Apple Preserve

This recipe makes a pleasant, sweet and fruity chutney that is not overpowering or excessively thick and heavy. Care needs to be taken during the final boiling process to ensure that the mixture does not 'catch' on the base of the pan, but the result is well worthwhile.

Ingredients for 2 medium sized jars:

450g/1lb beetroot, peeled and grated
1 large cooking apple, peeled, cored and
    grated
1 onion, finely chopped
50g/2oz light muscovado sugar
225ml/8fl oz white wine vinegar

MAKES ABOUT 2 JARS

Place the beetroot in a heavy-based pan with the apple, onion, sugar and vinegar. Bring to the boil, then reduce the heat and simmer for 40-45 minutes until the beetroot and apple are completely tender and the preserve is nicely reduced. Leave to cool a little, then spoon into sterilised jars, seal and label. Use as required.

Béchamel Sauce

This classic white sauce is the basis for so many dishes that it really is worth mastering. For a quicker version omit the first paragraph and continue as described below. Add a splash of cream just before serving to lift the flavours and give the finished sauce a creamy richness.

450ml/3/4 pint milk
1 small onion, roughly chopped
1 bay leaf
1/2 tsp black peppercorns
25g/1oz butter
25g/1oz plain flour
pinch of freshly grated nutmeg
salt and freshly grated pepper

MAKES ABOUT 450ML/3/4 PINT

Place the milk in a pan with the onion, bay leaf and peppercorns. Bring just to boiling point, then remove from the heat, cover and set aside to infuse for at least 10 and up to 30 minutes Strain through a sieve into a jug.

Wipe out the pan and use to melt the butter. Stir in the flour and cook for 1 minute, stirring. Remove from the heat and gradually pour in the infused milk, whisking until smooth after each addition. Season to taste and add a pinch of nutmeg.

Bring the sauce to the boil, whisking constantly, then reduce the heat and simmer gently for 5 minutes until smooth and thickened, stirring occasionally. Use as required or transfer to a jug, cover with clingfilm and keep in the fridge for up to 2 days.

VARIATIONS

CHEESE SAUCE
When the sauce is cooked, remove from the heat and stir in 50g/2oz of freshly grated Parmesan until melted.

PARSLEY SAUCE
When the sauce is cooked, remove from the heat and stir in 2 tablespoons of chopped fresh flat-leaf parsley.

CREAMY MUSTARD SAUCE
Reduce the milk by 150ml/1/4 pint and make the sauce as described above. Once the sauce is cooked, stir in the cream and add a tablespoon of Dijon mustard, then simmer gently for a minute or two, whisking to combine.

ONION SAUCE
Sauté 1 finely chopped onion in 25g/1oz of butter for 10-15 minutes until completely softened but not coloured. Whisk into the cooked sauce and whizz with a hand-blender if you like a smooth finish.

Mayonnaise

This quick mayonnaise is made in a food processor and it will keep happily in the fridge for up to one week. It literally takes minutes to make and is far superior to any shop bought alternatives.

1 egg, at room temperature
2 tsp white wine vinegar
½ tsp salt
pinch of caster sugar
1 tsp Dijon mustard
120ml/4fl oz olive oil
120ml/4fl oz sunflower oil

MAKES 300ML/¹/₂ PINT

Break the egg into the food processor and add the vinegar, salt, sugar, mustard and half of the olive oil. Secure the lid and whizz for 10 seconds. Leave to stand for a couple of seconds, then turn on again at medium speed and pour the remaining olive oil and sunflower oil through the feeder tube in a thin steady stream. This should take 25-30 seconds. Switch off the machine, take off the lid, scrape down the sides, and whizz again for 2-3 seconds. Transfer to a bowl or a jar, season to taste and cover with clingfilm. Chill until ready to use.

VARIATIONS

LEMON AND DILL
Stir the finely grated rind of 1 lemon and 2 tablespoons of chopped fresh dill into the mayonnaise.

BASIL
Add a good handful of fresh basil leaves to the food processor with the egg and continue to make as described above.

Sweet Mustard Dressing

This is actually a version of a classic mayonnaise but is thinner and tastes wonderfully sweet with a mustardy tang. It is perfect served with all types of cold smoked fish or as part of a large mixed smoked fish platter (page 155).

2 tbsp Dijon mustard
1 tbsp caster sugar
1 egg yolk
120ml/4fl oz sunflower oil
2 tbsp chopped fresh dill
salt and freshly ground black pepper

MAKES ABOUT 150ML/¹/₄ PINT

Place the mustard in a bowl with the sugar and egg yolk, then whisk to combine. Gradually add the oil, drop by drop to start with and then in a thin continuous stream, whisking constantly, until the dressing becomes thickened and smooth. Season and stir in half of the dill, then cover and chill until ready to use.

Hollandaise Sauce

This sauce is wonderful served with char-grilled fish or poached salmon (page 168). If you add in a teaspoon each of vinegar and tarragon, you've got **Béarnaise Sauce**, which is great served with seafood.

2 egg yolks
1 egg
pinch of salt
225g/8oz unsalted butter

MAKES ABOUT 450ML/ $^3/_4$ PINT

Place the egg yolks and egg into a food processor with the salt. Blend until just combined.

Gently heat the butter in a heavy-based pan until melted and just beginning to foam. Turn on the food processor and with the motor running at medium speed; pour in the melted butter in a thin, steady stream through the feeder tube. Continue to blend for another 5 seconds and pour back into the pan but do not return to the heat.

Allow the heat from the pan to finish thickening the sauce as you stir it gently for another minute before serving. Alternatively, the sauce can be kept warm if it's kept in a heatproof bowl set over a pan of simmering water or in a switched-off but warm oven.

Beurre Blanc

This version of the classic sauce includes stock; as stock cubes are too salty, you need to make your own, or use the cartons of chilled stocks available in most supermarkets. Alternatively, make the stock-free version (see below).

600ml/1 pint chicken or vegetable stock
225g/8oz unsalted butter, diced and
    chilled
juice of ½ lemon
salt and freshly ground black pepper

MAKES ABOUT 300ML/ $^1/_2$ PINT

Place the chicken or vegetable stock in a pan and reduce to about 50ml/2fl oz. This should take about 10 minutes. Reduce the heat right down and whisk in the butter a few cubes at a time (or use a hand blender) until the butter has melted and the texture is light and frothy. Add a squeeze of lemon juice and season to taste.

VARIATION
In a small heavy pan, boil 45ml/3 tbsp each of white wine vinegar and dry white wine with 2 finely chopped shallots. Add 1 tbsp double cream/crème fraîche if liked, and re-boil to a glaze. Gradually whisk in 225g/8oz very cold butter, cubed, to make a creamy sauce. Finally, bring just to a boil over high heat, whisking continuously. Strain if liked, season to taste and serve.

Mustard & Dill Sauce

Traditionally, this sauce is served with gravadlax, the Scandinavian alternative to smoked salmon, but it could also be used as a dressing for a warm salad with some poached smoked haddock and a poached egg.

2 tbsp Dijon mustard
1 tbsp caster sugar
1 tbsp white wine vinegar
1 egg yolk
150ml/¼ pint groundnut or
　　vegetable oil
1 tbsp chopped fresh dill
salt and freshly ground black pepper

MAKES ABOUT 200ML/7FL OZ

Place the mustard, sugar, vinegar and egg yolk in a large bowl and whisk to combine. Add the oil drop by drop to begin with, then in a steady stream, whisking constantly, until the sauce becomes thick and smooth. Stir in the dill and season to taste. Cover with clingfilm and chill until needed.

French Vinaigrette

This is an excellent version of French vinaigrette, but you can adapt it to your own personal taste by using red or white wine vinegar, or experiment with different oils. This makes enough to dress a good-sized green or mixed salad.

1 tbsp white wine vinegar
pinch of caster sugar
4 tbsp extra virgin olive oil
½ tsp Dijon mustard
1 small garlic clove, crushed
salt and freshly ground black pepper

SERVES 4-6
MAKES ABOUT 75ML/3FL OZ

Place the vinegar in a screw-topped jar and add the sugar and a good pinch of salt, then shake until the salt has dissolved. Add the oil to the jar with the mustard and garlic and shake again until you have formed a thick emulsion. Season to taste and chill until needed.

VARIATIONS

MUSTARD VINAIGRETTE
Increase the Dijon mustard to 1 teaspoon, then add with 1 teaspoon of wholegrain mustard and 1 tablespoon of snipped fresh chives.

BALSAMIC AND HONEY DRESSING
Replace the white wine vinegar with balsamic and the sugar with ½ a teaspoon of honey. Omit the Dijon mustard.

CREAMY GARLIC DRESSING
Whisk in a tablespoon of mayonnaise (home-made page 202 or shop bought).

Vegetable Stock

If time allows, vegetable stock is best marinated for two days to allow the flavours to really infuse and develop. It gives you a fuller vegetable flavour and is definitely worth the wait. It freezes well in small tubs so that you can defrost the required quantity as and when you need it.

2 leeks, finely chopped
2 onions, finely chopped
2 carrots, cut into 1cm/½ inch dice
2 celery sticks, finely chopped
1 fennel bulb, cut into 1 cm/½ inch dice
1 head garlic, sliced in half crossways
1 fresh thyme sprig
1 bay leaf
1 tsp pink peppercorns
1 tsp coriander seeds
1 star anise
pinch of salt

MAKES ABOUT 1.2 LITRES/2 PINTS

Place all of the ingredients in a large pan and cover with 1.75 litres/3 pints of water. Bring to a simmer and then cook for another 30 minutes until the vegetables are tender. Either set aside to marinate for 2 days in a cool place, or if you're short of time, strain through a sieve. Taste. If you find the flavour is not full enough, return to the pan and reduce until you are happy. Use as required or freeze in 600ml/1 pint cartons, and defrost when you need it.

Chicken Stock

This chicken stock is much more versatile than any other stock and it makes the perfect base for soups, stews and sauces. It freezes very well, so always try to make a pot when having a roast chicken for dinner.

1 large chicken carcass, skin and fat
    removed and chopped
2 leeks, chopped
2 onions, chopped
2 carrots, chopped
2 celery sticks, chopped
1 fresh thyme sprig
1 bay leaf
handful fresh parsley stalks
1 tsp white peppercorns

MAKES ABOUT 1.2 LITRES/2 PINTS

Place the chicken carcass in a large pan and cover with 1.8 litres/3¼ pints of water. Bring to the boil, then skim off any fat and scum from the surface. Reduce the heat to a simmer and tip in all of the remaining ingredients.

Simmer gently for another 2-3 hours, skimming occasionally and tasting regularly to check the flavour. When you are happy with it, remove from the heat and pass through a sieve. Leave to cool and remove any fat that settles on the top, then use as required or freeze in 600ml/1 pint cartons, and defrost when you need it.

Fish Stock

Lemon sole, brill and plaice bones make a wonderful, almost sweet fish stock. It is fine to include heads and bones and skin of most types of fish, but avoid salmon, red mullet and oil-rich fish. When the stock is made, you can reduce it further and then freeze it in ice cube trays (freezing it this way means you can defrost as little or as much as you need at a time).

250g/9oz fish trimmings
3 leeks, chopped
1 bulb fennel, chopped
3 carrots, chopped
large handful fresh parsley, roughly
    chopped
175ml/6fl oz dry white wine

MAKES ABOUT 1.2 LITRES/2 PINTS

Rinse the fish bones and trimmings of any blood, which would make the stock look cloudy and taste bitter. Place into a large heavy-bottomed stockpot with the leeks, fennel, carrots and parsley. Pour in the white wine, then add enough cold water to cover the fish and vegetables, (but no more than 1.2 litres/2 pints). Place on a high heat and bring to a simmer. After 5 minutes, remove the scum that forms on the surface with a spoon and discard. Reduce the heat and simmer, covered, for about 25 minutes, skimming as necessary.

At the end of cooking time, remove the stock from the heat and strain, discarding the fish trimmings and the vegetables. Cool and store in the fridge for up to 3 days or freeze.

US Conversions - Guidelines

TABLESPOONS
1 tablespoon = 1¼ US tablespoons
2 tablespoons = 2½ US tablespoons
3 tablespoons = 3¾ US tablespoons
4 tablespoons = 5 US tablespoons

BUTTER
25g = 2 tbsp = ¼ stick
100g = 8 tbsp = 1 stick

CHEESE
Grated 115g = 1 cup
Cream cheese 225g = 1 cup

DRIED FRUIT
Raisins, sultanas 150g = 1 cup
Glacé cherries, etc 125g = 1 cup

FISH
Prawns, peeled 175g = 1 cup
Cooked and flaked 225g = 1 cup

FLOUR
Firmly packed 115g = 1 cup

LIQUIDS
Water, etc 225ml = 1 cup
150ml = ¾ cup
300ml = 1⅓ cups
500ml = 2¼ cups
600ml = 2¾ cups
900ml = 1½ pints/4 cups
Syrup, honey 350g = 1 cup

NUTS
Almonds, whole/shelled 150g = 1 cup
Almonds, flaked 115g = 1 cup
Ground nuts 115g = 1 cup

OATS
Rolled oats 100g = 1 cup
Oatmeal 175g = 1 cup

PULSES
Lentils 225g = 1 cup

RICE
Uncooked 200g = 1 cup
Cooked and drained 165g = 1 cup

SUGAR
Caster and granulated 225g = 1 cup
Moist brown 200g = 1 cup
Icing sugar 125g = 1 cup

VEGETABLES
Onions, chopped 115g = 1 cup
Cabbage, shredded 75g = 1 cup
Peas, shelled 150g = 1 cup
Beansprouts 50g = 1 cup
Potatoes, peeled & diced 170g = 1 cup
Potatoes, mashed 225g = 1 cup
Tomatoes 225g = 1 cup

Index